Better Homes and Gardens®

MICROWAVE
COOKING FOR ONE OR TWO

© Copyright 1983 by Meredith Corporation, Des Moines, Iowa.
All Rights Reserved. Printed in the United States of America.
First Edition. Seventh Printing, 1987.
Library of Congress Catalog Card Number: 82-61519
ISBN: 0-696-01160-3

On the cover:
Lamb and Vegetable Combo (see recipe, page 90)

BETTER HOMES AND GARDENS® BOOKS
Editor: Gerald M. Knox
Art Director: Ernest Shelton
Managing Editor: David A. Kirchner

Food and Nutrition Editor: Doris Eby
Department Head—Cook Books: Sharyl Heiken
Senior Food Editors: Rosemary C. Hutchinson, Elizabeth Woolever
Senior Associate Food Editor: Sandra Granseth
Associate Food Editors: Jill Burmeister, Linda Foley, Linda Henry,
    Julia Malloy, Alethea Sparks, Marcia Stanley, Diane Yanney
Recipe Development Editor: Marion Viall
Test Kitchen Director: Sharon Stilwell
Test Kitchen Home Economists: Jean Brekke, Kay Cargill,
    Marilyn Cornelius, Maryellyn Krantz, Dianna Nolin, Marge Steenson

Associate Art Directors (Creative): Linda Ford, Neoma Alt West
Associate Art Director (Managing): Randall Yontz
Copy and Production Editors: Marsha Jahns,
    Nancy Nowiszewski, Mary Helen Schiltz, David A. Walsh
Assistant Art Directors: Harijs Priekulis, Tom Wegner
Graphic Designers: Mike Burns, Trish Church-Podlasek, Alisann Dixon,
    Mike Eagleton, Lynda Haupert, Deb Miner, Lyne Neymeyer,
    Stan Sams, D. Greg Thompson, Darla Whipple, Paul Zimmerman

Editor in Chief: Neil Kuehnl
Group Editorial Services Director: Duane L. Gregg

General Manager: Fred Stines
Director of Publishing: Robert B. Nelson
Director of Retail Marketing: Jamie Martin
Director of Direct Marketing: Arthur Heydendael

Microwave Cooking for One or Two
Editors: Linda Foley, Marcia Stanley
Copy and Production Editor: Marsha Jahns
Graphic Designers: Trish Church-Podlasek, Deb Miner

Our seal assures you that every recipe in
Microwave Cooking for One or Two
has been tested in the Better Homes and
Gardens Test Kitchen. This means that
each recipe is practical and reliable, and
meets our high standards of taste appeal.

CONTENTS

ALL ABOUT MICROWAVE COOKING

What do you do when you usually cook for one or two and you love the speed and convenience of a microwave oven, but all of your microwave cook books contain only recipes that make four, six, or more servings? The editors of Better Homes and Gardens have a solution to this difficult problem—microwave recipes that make one or two servings.

To get you started on micro-cooking in small quantities, this first section, All About Microwave Cooking, explains the basics. It tells what variable power means and which utensils you can use for micro-cooking. In addition, it gives you three special charts—Reheating Foods for One or Two, Defrosting Foods for One or Two, and Microwave Tips.

In the three chapters that follow you'll find delicious ideas and specific instructions for many micro-cooked foods for one or two. The first chapter contains 49 special recipes that give quantities and cooking times for both one and two servings. In the second chapter you'll find recipes that help you turn the smallest common unit of food you can buy into several different and exciting recipes. And the third chapter contains microwave versions of favorite one-dish meals for one or two.

- Use chapter 1 recipes to prepare Sausage and Cornbread Cabbage Rolls and Carrots in Orange-Basil Butter (see recipes, pages 24 and 42).

- One of four recipes from chapter 2 designed to use an entire package of ground beef is Meatball Sandwiches (see recipe, page 63).

- Lamb and Vegetable Combo is one of the many easy-to-prepare one-dish meals from chapter 3 (see recipe, page 90).

MICROWAVE COOKWARE FOR ONE OR TWO

When micro-cooking small quantities of food, as in one- or two-serving recipes, it's especially important to use the right utensils. A small amount of food in a large dish will not micro-cook properly. However, this doesn't mean that you have to purchase lots of new dishes. You probably can use many of the dishes you already own.

For example, such standard kitchen items as custard cups of various sizes, 1- and 2-cup glass measures, nonmetal coffee mugs, nonmetal soup bowls, and 1-, 1½-, and 2-quart nonmetal casseroles are all commonly used in micro-cooking for one or two people. What you may want to consider purchasing are some of the smaller-sized utensils, such as a 15-ounce casserole, a 20-ounce casserole, a 7-inch pie plate, a 4½-inch pie plate or quiche dish, or a 6½-inch browning dish. Take a quick inventory of your dishes and look through the recipes in this book to determine which dishes you may want to add to your kitchen supplies.

When selecting new microwave cookware or deciding if you can use one of your dishes in the microwave oven, keep the following guidelines in mind.
• If the manufacturer has labeled the dish or utensil microwave-safe or suitable for microwaving, you should have no problem using it for micro-cooking. If the dish or utensil is not labeled, consider the type of material from which the dish or utensil is made.
• If the dish is paper, you can use it to micro-cook foods on 100% power for as long as 4 minutes. However, never use a paper dish for a longer cooking time or with very small quantities of food (less than ¼ cup) because it could catch fire.

Choose undyed paper products, because the dyes on colored paper can leak onto the food. Look for products that are labeled as microwave-safe, then follow the manufacturer's instructions.
• If the utensil is metal, first check your microwave oven owner's manual to see if your oven is one in which metal can be used. If it is, the amount of metal you can use probably will depend on the amount of food you are micro-cooking. For example, a foil tray should be at least ⅔ to ¾ full. Also, never allow any metal to touch the sides or top of your microwave oven because it could damage the microwave oven.
• If the container is plastic, it probably can be used in your microwave oven. However, plastic utensils do vary in the food temperatures that they can withstand, so be sure to read the utensil manufacturer's directions carefully and use the dish as recommended.
• Finally, if the dish is made of glass, china, or pottery, you'll need to test the dish to see if you can use it in your microwave oven. To test a dish, pour ½ cup of cold water into a glass measure. Set it in the oven, inside or beside the dish you wish to test. Micro-cook on 100% power for 1 minute. If the water is warm but the dish remains cool, the dish can be used for micro-cooking. If the water is warm and the dish feels lukewarm, the dish is suitable for heating or reheating food, but probably not for micro-cooking food. If the water stays cool and the dish becomes hot, do not use the dish. Also, do not use a dish or plate that has gold or silver trim or markings. The metal in the trim or markings may blacken or overheat the area next to it and crack the dish.

VARIABLE POWER

If your microwave oven has more power settings than on and off, it has variable power. Variable power means that you can micro-cook foods at power settings other than 100% power—such as 10% power, 30% power, 50% power, and 70% power.

Microwave ovens with variable power achieve power settings lower than 100% by cycling microwave energy on and off during the micro-cooking time. The periods of off energy help to equalize the cooking of many foods. Most of the newer microwave ovens have variable power with anywhere from two to ten different power settings. The settings on microwave ovens and the percent of power assigned to these settings by the manufacturer vary by brand of microwave oven; therefore, before you do any micro-cooking you need to find out which setting on your microwave oven corresponds to what percentage of power.

If your microwave oven has numbered settings, this is easy to determine. For example, a setting of 10 corresponds to 100% power, a setting of 5 corresponds to 50% power, and a setting of 1 corresponds to 10% power. However, if your microwave has named settings, such as high, medium, defrost, or roast, you'll have to use the following test to determine percentages of power on your microwave oven.

In a 4-cup measure combine 1 cup cold tap water and 8 ice cubes. Stir the cold water and ice cubes for 1 minute. Pour off 1 cup of the water into a 1-cup measure and discard the ice cubes and any remaining water. Micro-cook the water, uncovered, on 100% power or the highest possible named setting till it reaches a full boil. This should take 3 to 4 minutes. Watch the water and time it carefully. Discard the hot water and let both of the measuring cups return to room temperature.

Repeat the procedure with fresh water and ice cubes, using the setting you wish to test. If the water takes approximately twice as long to boil, the setting is 50% power. If the water boils in *less* than twice the time, the setting is *higher* than 50% power; or if the water boils in *more* than twice the time, the setting is *lower* than 50% power.

You'll find that most recipes in this book call for a 100% power setting or a 50% power setting. If your microwave oven has only one power setting other than 100% power, test it, as described above, to see if it might actually be 50% power. If you find that the setting is higher than 50% power, you should not use it for recipes requiring 50% power or less. But if you find that it is less than 50% power, you can use it for recipes calling for 50% power. Just use your microwave oven's lower power setting in place of the 50% power and plan on the food taking the maximum time or a little longer to micro-cook.

DEFROSTING FOODS FOR ONE OR TWO

When you're short on time and dinner's in the freezer, you can still serve the delicious meal you planned—without waiting hours for it to thaw. Microwave defrosting is the answer. Your microwave oven makes thawing fast, easy, and convenient. All you have to do to defrost foods for one or two is follow the timings and directions on this chart.

FOOD	AMOUNT
Bread	2 slices 4 slices
Bread dough	1 16-ounce loaf
Roll dough	2 rolls 4 rolls
Butter or margarine	½ stick 1 stick
Ground beef, pork, or lamb	¼ pound ½ pound
Chops and steaks	½ pound (1 inch thick)
Bacon	2 slices 4 slices ½ pound (about 11 slices)
Cut-up chicken pieces	¼ pound ½ pound
Shrimp	¼ pound ½ pound
Lobster tail	1 8-ounce tail 2 8-ounce tails
Meat-vegetable casserole	1 cup 2 cups
Vegetables	½ of a 9- or 10-ounce package
Soup	1 cup 2 cups

POWER	TIME	METHOD
30% 30%	20 to 40 seconds 40 seconds to 1 minute	Stack bread slices on a nonmetal plate. Micro-cook, uncovered.
10%	15 to 17 minutes	Place the frozen bread dough in a lightly greased 8x4x2-inch loaf dish. Micro-cook, loosely covered, turning the loaf over once.
10% 10%	2½ to 3½ minutes 3½ to 4½ minutes	Place the frozen roll dough in a lightly greased shallow baking dish. Micro-cook, loosely covered.
30% 30%	about 1 minute 1 to 1½ minutes	Unwrap and place on a nonmetal plate. Micro-cook, uncovered.
30% 30%	1½ to 3 minutes 2½ to 4½ minutes	Unwrap ground meat and place in a small nonmetal dish or casserole. Micro-cook, loosely covered, rotating dish a quarter-turn once.
30%	about 5 minutes	Unwrap and place in a shallow baking dish. Micro-cook, loosely covered, turning once. Let stand 10 minutes.
30% 30% 30%	30 seconds to 1 minute 1 to 1½ minutes 1½ to 2½ minutes	Place bacon on a nonmetal plate or in a baking dish. Micro-cook, loosely covered.
30% 30%	2 to 3 minutes 3 to 4 minutes	Unwrap and place in a shallow baking dish. Micro-cook, loosely covered, rearranging once.
30% 30%	2 to 3 minutes 3 to 5 minutes	In a shallow baking dish micro-cook, loosely covered, rearranging once.
30% 30%	3 to 5 minutes 5 to 8 minutes	Unwrap lobster tail(s) and place in a baking dish. Micro-cook, uncovered, till flexible. Let stand 5 minutes.
30% 30%	6 to 8 minutes 8 to 12 minutes	Unwrap frozen casserole mixture. In a nonmetal dish micro-cook, uncovered, stirring once. Do not freeze a flour- or cornstarch-thickened casserole.
30%	2 to 3½ minutes	Place vegetables in a small nonmetal dish or casserole. Micro-cook, uncovered, stirring once.
30% 30%	5 to 8 minutes 8 to 12 minutes	Unwrap frozen soup. In a nonmetal bowl or casserole micro-cook, uncovered, stirring once. Do not freeze a flour- or cornstarch-thickened soup.

Reheating Foods for One or Two

Microwave ovens are great for reheating foods. They not only allow you to warm foods in a short amount of time, but also to serve reheated meals without sacrificing flavor and texture. With a microwave oven it doesn't matter whether you make a dish in advance or serve leftovers, the food will still be fresh-tasting. To reheat cooked foods for one or two, use this simple chart.

FOOD	AMOUNT
Beverage	1 6-ounce serving 2 6-ounce servings
Muffins	1 muffin 2 muffins 4 muffins
French bread	¼ of a 1-pound loaf
Bread stuffing	½ cup 1 cup
Rice or pasta	½ cup 1 cup
Meat-vegetable casserole	1 cup 2 cups
Casserole containing sour cream or yogurt	1 cup 2 cups
Flour- or cornstarch-thickened sauce	¼ cup ½ cup
Egg-thickened sauce	¼ cup ½ cup
Barbecue-type or soup-based sauce	¼ cup ½ cup
Sauce containing sour cream or yogurt	¼ cup ½ cup
Soup	1 cup 2 cups
Cut-up vegetables	½ cup 1 cup
Mashed vegetables	½ cup 1 cup
Fruit pie	1 slice (⅛ pie) 2 slices (⅛ pie each)

POWER	TIME	METHOD
100% 100%	1¼ to 1½ minutes 2½ to 3 minutes	Pour chilled beverage into nonmetal cup(s) or mug(s). Micro-cook, uncovered.
100% 100% 100%	8 to 12 seconds 12 to 18 seconds 30 to 50 seconds	Wrap muffin(s) loosely in a napkin or paper towel.
100%	15 to 25 seconds	Place in a small brown paper bag; sprinkle bag lightly with water.
100% 100%	about 30 seconds about 1 minute	For ½ cup stuffing, stir in ½ teaspoon water; for 1 cup stuffing, stir in 1 teaspoon water. In a nonmetal dish micro-cook, covered.
70% 70%	1½ to 2 minutes 2½ to 3 minutes	For ½ cup rice or pasta, stir in 1 teaspoon water; for 1 cup rice or pasta, stir in 2 teaspoons water. In a nonmetal dish micro-cook, covered.
70% 70%	3½ to 4 minutes 7 to 8 minutes	In a nonmetal dish micro-cook, covered.
50% 50%	4 to 5 minutes 9 to 10 minutes	In a nonmetal dish micro-cook, covered.
50% 50%	about 1 minute about 2 minutes	In a nonmetal dish micro-cook, uncovered, stirring every 30 seconds.
50% 50%	about 1 minute about 2 minutes	In a nonmetal dish micro-cook, uncovered, stirring every 30 seconds.
100% 100%	45 to 50 seconds 1¼ to 1½ minutes	In a nonmetal dish micro-cook, uncovered, stirring every 30 seconds.
50% 50%	about 1 minute about 2 minutes	In a nonmetal dish micro-cook, uncovered, stirring every 30 seconds.
70% 70%	4 to 4½ minutes 5 to 5½ minutes	In a nonmetal dish micro-cook, loosely covered.
100% 100%	1 to 1½ minutes 1½ to 2 minutes	In a nonmetal dish micro-cook, covered.
70% 70%	1 to 1½ minutes 1½ to 2 minutes	For ½ cup mashed vegetables, stir in 1 teaspoon water; for 1 cup mashed vegetables, stir in 2 teaspoons water. In a nonmetal dish micro-cook, covered.
70% 70%	45 seconds to 1 minute 1 to 1½ minutes	Place on nonmetal plate(s); micro-cook, uncovered.

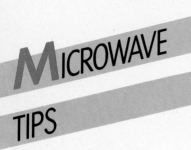

MICROWAVE TIPS

Even if you don't use your microwave oven to prepare an entire recipe, you'll find it a timesaving convenience. Use it to shorten some of the preliminary chores in a recipe, such as melting butter or chocolate, toasting nuts or coconut, plumping dried fruit, or softening cream cheese. On these two pages you'll find directions and timings for these and many other recipe shortcuts.

Toasting nuts: Place ½ cup of the desired nuts in a 2-cup measure. Micro-cook, uncovered, on 100% power about 3 minutes or till toasted, stirring frequently.

Blanching almonds: In a small nonmetal bowl micro-cook 1 cup water, uncovered, on 100% power for 2 to 3 minutes or till boiling. Add ½ cup almonds to water. Micro-cook, uncovered, on 100% power for 1½ minutes. Drain; rinse almonds with cold water. Slip off skins.

Toasting coconut: Place flaked or shredded coconut in a 1-cup measure. Micro-cook, uncovered, on 100% power till light brown, stirring every 20 seconds. Allow 1 to 1½ minutes for ¼ cup or 1½ to 2 minutes for ½ cup coconut.

Warming ice cream toppers: Spoon topping into a custard cup or 1-cup measure. Micro-cook, uncovered, on 100% power till warm, allowing about 15 seconds for 2 tablespoons, about 25 seconds for ¼ cup, or about 45 seconds for ½ cup topping.

Softening ice cream: Micro-cook 1 pint solidly frozen ice cream, uncovered, on 100% power about 15 seconds or till soft enough to serve.

Plumping dried fruit: In a 2-cup measure micro-cook 1 cup water, uncovered, on 100% power for 2 to 3 minutes or till boiling. Stir in ½ cup desired dried fruit. Let stand for 5 to 10 minutes; drain.

Softening butter or margarine: Unwrap butter or margarine and place in a small nonmetal dish. Micro-cook, uncovered, on 10% power, allowing about 30 seconds for 2 tablespoons or 50 seconds to 1 minute for ¼ cup butter or margarine.

Melting butter or margarine: Unwrap butter or margarine and place in a 1-cup measure or custard cup. Micro-cook, uncovered, on 100% power, allowing 25 to 30 seconds for 2 tablespoons or about 40 seconds for ¼ cup butter or margarine.

Softening cream cheese: Unwrap one 3-ounce package cream cheese and place in a small nonmetal bowl. Micro-cook, uncovered, on 30% power about 1 minute or till soft.

Melting chocolate squares: Unwrap chocolate and place in a small nonmetal bowl or custard cup. Micro-cook, uncovered, on 100% power till melted, stirring once. Allow 1½ to 1¾ minutes for one 1-ounce square or 1¾ to 2 minutes for two 1-ounce squares chocolate.

Melting chocolate pieces: In a glass measure or custard cup micro-cook chocolate pieces, uncovered, on 100% power till melted, stirring once. Allow 1 to 1½ minutes for ½ of a 6-ounce package (½ cup) or 1½ to 2 minutes for one 6-ounce package (1 cup) chocolate pieces.

Melting confectioner's coating: In a small nonmetal bowl or custard cup micro-cook confectioner's coating, uncovered, on 100% power till melted, stirring once. Allow 1 to 1¼ minutes for one 2-ounce square or about 1½ minutes for two 2-ounce squares confectioner's coating.

Melting caramels: Unwrap caramels and place in a glass measure. Micro-cook, uncovered, on 100% power till melted, stirring once. Allow 45 seconds to 1 minute for 14 caramels (about ½ cup) or 1 to 1½ minutes for 28 caramels (about 1 cup).

Flaming liqueur: Place 2 tablespoons desired liqueur or liquor (at least 80 proof) in a 1-cup measure. Micro-cook, uncovered, on 100% power for 20 seconds. Ignite and pour over desired food.

Peeling tomatoes: In a 2-cup measure micro-cook 1 cup water, uncovered, on 100% power for 2 to 3 minutes or till boiling. Spear 1 tomato with a long-tined fork. Submerge into hot water; hold about 12 seconds. Place tomato under cold running water; slip off peel.

Peeling peaches: In a 2-cup measure micro-cook 1 cup water, uncovered, on 100% power for 2 to 3 minutes or till boiling. Spear 1 peach with a long-tined fork. Submerge into hot water; hold about 12 seconds. Place peach under cold running water; slip off peel.

Making croutons: Spread 2 cups of ½-inch bread cubes in a shallow baking dish. Micro-cook, uncovered, on 100% power for 3½ to 4½ minutes or till crisp and dry, stirring every 2 minutes.

Crisping snacks: Spread 1 cup stale chips, pretzels, crackers, or other snacks in a 7-inch pie plate or shallow baking dish. Micro-cook, uncovered, on 100% power for 30 to 45 seconds. Let stand 1 minute.

Precooking vegetables for kabobs or stir-fry: Place desired raw vegetable pieces of uniform size (carrots, zucchini, onions, new potatoes, cauliflower, asparagus, or broccoli) in a casserole. Add 1 tablespoon water. Micro-cook, covered, on 100% power till almost tender. Allow 45 seconds to 1 minute for ½ cup and 1½ to 2 minutes for 1 cup.

Reheating cocktail meatballs: Place meatballs and sauce in a 7-inch pie plate. Micro-cook, uncovered, on 100% power till warm, stirring once. Allow 1½ to 2 minutes for ½ cup or 2½ to 3 minutes for 1 cup.

Making quick appetizers: Arrange bread pieces, toast pieces, or crackers on a nonmetal serving plate lined with paper toweling. Top with desired spread. Micro-cook 7 to 9 appetizers at a time, uncovered, on 100% power about 20 seconds or till spread is hot.

Serving make-ahead cheese ball: Prepare desired 3- to 4-inch cheese ball; wrap in moisture-vaporproof wrap, seal, label, and freeze. Before serving, unwrap and place on a nonmetal serving plate. Micro-cook, uncovered, on 30% power for 5 minutes. Let stand 10 minutes.

Making quick mini yeast loaves: Place one 16-ounce loaf frozen bread dough in a lightly greased 8x4x2-inch loaf dish. Micro-cook, uncovered, on 10% power for 8 to 10 minutes or till thawed just enough to cut. Cut loaf into 6 equal portions. Return 4 or 5 portions to freezer. Continue thawing 1 or 2 portions by micro-cooking, loosely covered, on 10% power, allowing 4 to 5 minutes for 1 portion or 6 to 8 minutes for 2 portions bread dough. Following package directions, let rise. Bake in a conventional oven according to package directions.

RECIPES FOR ONE OR TWO

Whether you usually cook for one or typically cook for two, there are times when that pattern is varied.

To solve the problem of cooking for one when your usual meal partner is away, or the problem of cooking for two when you've invited a friend to dinner, we've given you both one-serving and two-serving versions of every recipe in this chapter. You'll find versatile recipes for *Sausage and Cornbread Cabbage Rolls, Carrots in* *Orange-Basil Butter,* and *Toasty Walnut Muffins,* as well as many other recipes for main dishes, side dishes, desserts, snacks, and beverages (see the Index for recipe pages). With these recipes you can cook for one or two people without the guesswork of adjusting recipe proportions and timings, and without ending up with lots of leftovers.

SAVORY HAMBURGER SOUP

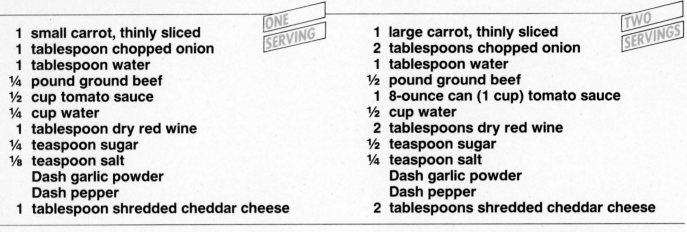

ONE SERVING	TWO SERVINGS
1 small carrot, thinly sliced	1 large carrot, thinly sliced
1 tablespoon chopped onion	2 tablespoons chopped onion
1 tablespoon water	1 tablespoon water
¼ pound ground beef	½ pound ground beef
½ cup tomato sauce	1 8-ounce can (1 cup) tomato sauce
¼ cup water	½ cup water
1 tablespoon dry red wine	2 tablespoons dry red wine
¼ teaspoon sugar	½ teaspoon sugar
⅛ teaspoon salt	¼ teaspoon salt
Dash garlic powder	Dash garlic powder
Dash pepper	Dash pepper
1 tablespoon shredded cheddar cheese	2 tablespoons shredded cheddar cheese

In a 20-ounce casserole micro-cook sliced carrot, chopped onion, and 1 tablespoon water, covered, on 100% power for 1½ minutes. Stir the ground beef into the partially cooked vegetables. Micro-cook, uncovered, on 100% power for 2 minutes, stirring once to break up the meat. Drain off fat.

Stir in tomato sauce, ¼ cup water, dry red wine, sugar, salt, garlic powder, and pepper. Micro-cook, uncovered, on 100% power for 2 to 3 minutes more or till mixture is heated through and vegetables are tender. Sprinkle with shredded cheddar cheese. Makes 1 serving.

In a 1-quart casserole micro-cook sliced carrot, chopped onion, and 1 tablespoon water, covered, on 100% power for 2 minutes. Stir the ground beef into the partially cooked vegetables. Micro-cook, uncovered, on 100% power for 3 minutes, stirring once to break up the meat. Drain off fat.

Stir in tomato sauce, ½ cup water, dry red wine, sugar, salt, garlic powder, and pepper. Micro-cook, uncovered, on 100% power for 4 to 5 minutes more or till mixture is heated through and vegetables are tender. Sprinkle with shredded cheddar cheese. Makes 2 servings.

STEAK AU POIVRE

ONE SERVING	TWO SERVINGS
½ teaspoon whole black peppercorns	1 teaspoon whole black peppercorns
1 beef cubed steak	2 beef cubed steaks
1 tablespoon cooking oil	2 tablespoons cooking oil
1 tablespoon brandy	2 tablespoons brandy
⅛ teaspoon instant beef bouillon granules	¼ teaspoon instant beef bouillon granules

Coarsely crack peppercorns. Sprinkle both sides of steak with crushed peppercorns, pressing in firmly with fingers. Let steak stand at room temperature for 30 minutes. Preheat a 6½-inch microwave browning dish on 100% power for 3 minutes. Add the cooking oil to the browning dish. Swirl to coat the dish.

Place the steak in the browning dish. Micro-cook, covered, on 100% power for 1 minute. Turn steak and micro-cook, covered, on 100% power about 30 seconds more or till done.

Remove steak to a warm plate. Stir brandy and bouillon granules into liquid in browning dish. Micro-cook, uncovered, on 100% power for 20 to 30 seconds or till boiling. Pour over steak. Makes 1 serving.

Coarsely crack peppercorns. Sprinkle both sides of steaks with crushed peppercorns, pressing in firmly with fingers. Let steak stand at room temperature for 30 minutes. Preheat a 10-inch microwave browning dish on 100% power for 3 minutes. Add the cooking oil to the browning dish. Swirl to coat the dish.

Place the steaks in the browning dish. Micro-cook, covered, on 100% power for 1 minute. Turn steaks and micro-cook, covered, on 100% power for 30 seconds to 1 minute more or till done.

Remove steaks to a warm serving platter. Stir brandy and bouillon granules into liquid in browning dish. Micro-cook, uncovered, on 100% power for 30 seconds to 1 minute or till boiling. Pour over steaks. Makes 2 servings.

SOUR CREAM BURGERS

ONE SERVING

2 tablespoons dairy sour cream
1 tablespoon sliced green onion
2 teaspoons fine dry bread crumbs
⅛ teaspoon salt
Dash pepper
¼ pound ground beef
1 hamburger bun, split, toasted, and buttered
Lettuce leaves
1 thin slice tomato
Dairy sour cream (optional)

Stir together 2 tablespoons sour cream, onion, bread crumbs, salt, and pepper. Add the ground beef; mix well. Shape the ground beef mixture into one ¾-inch-thick patty. Place the patty in a small baking dish. Loosely cover with clear plastic wrap or waxed paper. Micro-cook, loosely covered, on 100% power for 1½ minutes. Turn patty over; rotate the baking dish a half-turn. Micro-cook, loosely covered, on 100% power for 1½ to 2 minutes more or till done. Drain off fat. Serve on toasted bun with lettuce and tomato. Dollop with additional sour cream, if desired. Makes 1 serving.

TWO SERVINGS

¼ cup dairy sour cream
2 tablespoons sliced green onion
4 teaspoons fine dry bread crumbs
¼ teaspoon salt
Dash pepper
½ pound ground beef
2 hamburger buns, split, toasted, and buttered
Lettuce leaves
2 thin slices tomato
Dairy sour cream (optional)

Stir together ¼ cup sour cream, green onion, bread crumbs, salt, and pepper. Add the ground beef; mix well. Shape the ground beef mixture into two ¾-inch-thick patties. Place patties in a small baking dish. Loosely cover with clear plastic wrap or waxed paper. Micro-cook, loosely covered, on 100% power for 3 minutes. Turn patties over; rotate the baking dish a half-turn. Micro-cook, loosely covered, on 100% power for 2 to 3 minutes more or till done. Drain off fat. Serve the patties on toasted buns with lettuce and tomato. Dollop with additional sour cream, if desired. Makes 2 servings.

BEEF BURGUNDY STEW

ONE SERVING

1 slice bacon
2 teaspoons all-purpose flour
¼ teaspoon instant beef bouillon granules
⅛ teaspoon dried basil, crushed
¼ pound boneless beef stew meat, cut into ½-inch cubes
½ of a 7½-ounce can tomatoes, cut up
2 tablespoons dry red wine
¼ cup frozen pearl onions
4 small whole fresh mushrooms

In a 20-ounce casserole micro-cook bacon, loosely covered, on 100% power for 1 to 1½ minutes or till done. Drain bacon, reserving drippings in casserole. Crumble bacon and set aside. Stir flour, bouillon granules, and basil into drippings. Add beef, *undrained* tomatoes, and wine; mix well. Micro-cook, covered, on 100% power for 1 minute, stirring once. Micro-cook, covered, on 50% power for 10 minutes, stirring once. Stir in onions and mushrooms. Micro-cook, covered, on 50% power for 10 to 12 minutes or till meat is tender, stirring twice. Sprinkle crumbled bacon atop. Makes 1 serving.

TWO SERVINGS

2 slices bacon
4 teaspoons all-purpose flour
½ teaspoon instant beef bouillon granules
¼ teaspoon dried basil, crushed
½ pound boneless beef stew meat, cut into ½-inch cubes
1 7½-ounce can tomatoes, cut up
¼ cup dry red wine
½ cup frozen pearl onions
8 small whole fresh mushrooms

In a 1-quart casserole micro-cook bacon, loosely covered, on 100% power for 2 to 2½ minutes or till done. Drain bacon, reserving drippings in casserole. Crumble bacon and set aside. Stir flour, bouillon granules, and basil into drippings. Add beef, *undrained* tomatoes, and wine; mix well. Micro-cook, covered, on 100% power for 2 minutes, stirring once. Micro-cook, covered, on 50% power for 15 minutes, stirring twice. Stir in onions and mushrooms. Micro-cook, covered, on 50% power for 12 to 18 minutes or till meat and vegetables are tender, stirring twice. Sprinkle crumbled bacon atop. Makes 2 servings.

STUFFED STEAK ROLL

ONE SERVING	TWO SERVINGS
¼ **pound boneless beef top round steak, cut ½ inch thick**	½ **pound boneless beef top round steak, cut ½ inch thick**
2 **teaspoons water**	4 **teaspoons water**
1½ **teaspoons butter** *or* **margarine**	1 **tablespoon butter** *or* **margarine**
¼ **cup cornbread stuffing mix**	½ **cup cornbread stuffing mix**
1 **tablespoon shredded carrot**	2 **tablespoons shredded carrot**
1 **green onion, sliced**	2 **green onions, sliced**
½ **teaspoon water**	1 **teaspoon water**
½ **teaspoon Kitchen Bouquet**	1 **teaspoon Kitchen Bouquet**
1 **teaspoon butter** *or* **margarine**	2 **teaspoons butter** *or* **margarine**
1 **teaspoon all-purpose flour**	2 **teaspoons all-purpose flour**
¼ **cup water**	½ **cup water**
1 **teaspoon dry sherry**	2 **teaspoons dry sherry**
½ **teaspoon Kitchen Bouquet**	1 **teaspoon Kitchen Bouquet**
¼ **teaspoon instant beef bouillon granules**	½ **teaspoon instant beef bouillon granules**

Use a meat mallet to pound steak to ¼-inch thickness. In a 2-cup measure micro-cook 2 teaspoons water and 1½ teaspoons butter or margarine, uncovered, on 100% power about 30 seconds or till butter is melted. Stir in stuffing mix, carrot, and green onion. Spread mixture to within ½ inch of the edges of the meat. Roll up jelly-roll style starting at the narrow end. Tie steak roll with string or use wooden picks to secure. Place meat, seam side down, on a nonmetal rack in a shallow baking dish. Micro-cook, uncovered, on 50% power for 3 minutes.

Meanwhile, stir together ½ teaspoon water and ½ teaspoon Kitchen Bouquet. Brush over the meat roll. Turn the meat roll over. Brush again with Kitchen Bouquet mixture. Micro-cook, uncovered, on 50% power for 2 to 3 minutes more or till the meat is done, rotating the dish a half-turn once.

For the sauce, in a 2-cup measure micro-cook the 1 teaspoon butter or margarine, uncovered, on 100% power for 20 to 30 seconds or till melted. Stir in the flour. Add the ¼ cup water, sherry, ½ teaspoon Kitchen Bouquet, and beef bouillon granules; mix well. Micro-cook, uncovered, on 100% power for 1 to 2 minutes or till thickened and bubbly, stirring every 30 seconds. Slice meat roll into ½-inch-thick slices. Remove string or wooden picks. Serve sauce with meat. Makes 1 serving.

Use a meat mallet to pound steak to ¼-inch thickness. In a 2-cup measure micro-cook 4 teaspoons water and 1 tablespoon butter or margarine, uncovered, on 100% power about 45 seconds or till butter is melted. Stir in stuffing mix, carrot, and green onion. Spread mixture to within ½ inch of the edges of the meat. Roll up jelly-roll style starting at the narrow end. Tie steak roll with string or use wooden picks to secure. Place meat, seam side down, on a nonmetal rack in a shallow baking dish. Micro-cook, uncovered, on 50% power for 4 minutes.

Meanwhile, stir together 1 teaspoon water and 1 teaspoon Kitchen Bouquet. Brush over the meat roll. Turn the meat roll over. Brush again with Kitchen Bouquet mixture. Micro-cook, uncovered, on 50% power for 4 to 7 minutes more or till the meat is done, rotating the dish a half-turn every 2 minutes.

For the sauce, in a 2-cup measure micro-cook 2 teaspoons butter or margarine, uncovered, on 100% power for 30 to 45 seconds or till melted. Stir in the flour. Add the ½ cup water, sherry, 1 teaspoon Kitchen Bouquet, and beef bouillon granules; mix well. Micro-cook, uncovered, on 100% power for 1½ to 2½ minutes or till thickened and bubbly, stirring every 30 seconds. Slice meat roll into ½-inch-thick slices. Remove string or wooden picks. Serve sauce with meat. Makes 2 servings.

Filling and Rolling the Steak: Evenly spread the stuffing mixture over the steak to ½ inch of the edges. Roll up the steak jelly-roll style, beginning with a short edge. Tie the steak roll with string or secure with wooden picks.

Brushing the Steak Roll: Place the steak roll on a nonmetal rack in a shallow baking dish. During the micro-cooking of the steak roll, brush the surface of the steak with a mixture of Kitchen Bouquet and water. This will help enhance the brown color of the steak.

Serving the Steak Roll: Before you serve the stuffed steak roll, use a sharp knife to carefully slice the roll into ½-inch-thick slices. Be sure to remove the strings or wooden picks that were used to secure the roll during micro-cooking.

LASAGNA ROLLS

¼ **pound bulk Italian sausage**
2 **tablespoons chopped onion**
1 **beaten egg yolk**
¼ **cup cream-style cottage cheese**
1 **tablespoon grated**
 Parmesan cheese
2 **lasagna noodles, cooked**
½ **cup pizza sauce**
1½ **teaspoons water** *or* **dry red wine**
2 **tablespoons shredded**
 mozzarella cheese

½ **pound bulk Italian sausage**
¼ **cup chopped onion**
1 **beaten egg**
½ **cup cream-style cottage cheese**
2 **tablespoons grated**
 Parmesan cheese
4 **lasagna noodles, cooked**
1 **8-ounce can (1 cup) pizza sauce**
1 **tablespoon water** *or* **dry red wine**
¼ **cup shredded mozzarella cheese**

Crumble the Italian sausage into a 15-ounce casserole. Stir in the onion. Micro-cook, uncovered, on 100% power for 2 to 3 minutes or till the sausage is done and the onion is tender. Drain off the fat. Stir in the beaten egg yolk, cream-style cottage cheese, and grated Parmesan cheese.

Spread each lasagna noodle with some of the meat-cheese mixture. Roll up each noodle jelly-roll style, starting with the short edge. Place seam side down in a small greased baking dish.

Stir together the pizza sauce and water or dry red wine. Pour atop the lasagna rolls in the baking dish. Micro-cook, covered, on 100% power for 2 to 3 minutes or till the lasagna rolls are heated through. Sprinkle shredded mozzarella cheese atop the lasagna rolls. Micro-cook, uncovered, on 100% power about 30 seconds more or till the cheese is just melted. Makes 1 serving.

Crumble the Italian sausage into a 1-quart casserole. Stir in the onion. Micro-cook, uncovered, on 100% power for 3 to 4 minutes or till the sausage is done and the onion is tender. Drain off the fat. Stir in the beaten egg, cream-style cottage cheese, and grated Parmesan cheese.

Spread each lasagna noodle with some of the meat-cheese mixture. Roll up each noodle jelly-roll style, starting with the short edge. Place seam side down in a small greased baking dish.

Stir together the pizza sauce and water or dry red wine. Pour atop the lasagna rolls in the baking dish. Micro-cook, covered, on 100% power for 4 to 5 minutes or till the lasagna rolls are heated through. Sprinkle shredded mozzarella cheese atop the lasagna rolls. Micro-cook, uncovered, on 100% power for 30 seconds to 1 minute more or till the cheese is just melted. Makes 2 servings.

•
Making Lasagna Rolls is
a fun activity for the
young cook in your
home, who will require
only a little adult help.

TACO SALAD

¼ pound bulk pork sausage
1 tablespoon chopped onion
¼ cup tomato sauce
1 tablespoon chopped canned
    green chili peppers
¾ teaspoon all-purpose flour
½ teaspoon chili powder
    Dash garlic powder
1½ cups torn lettuce
1 small carrot, shredded
¼ cup cherry tomatoes, halved
2 tablespoons shredded Monterey Jack
    cheese
2 tablespoons coarsely crushed taco chips

Crumble pork sausage into a 15-ounce casserole. Stir in onion. Micro-cook, uncovered, on 100% power about 3 minutes or till the meat is no longer pink, stirring once. Drain off fat.

Stir in tomato sauce, canned green chili peppers, flour, chili powder, and garlic powder. Micro-cook, covered, on 100% power for 1 to 2 minutes or till slightly thickened and bubbly.

Meanwhile, in an individual salad bowl toss together lettuce, carrot, and tomatoes. Top with sausage mixture, cheese, and taco chips. Makes 1 serving.

½ pound bulk pork sausage
2 tablespoons chopped onion
½ cup tomato sauce
2 tablespoons chopped canned
    green chili peppers
1½ teaspoons all-purpose flour
1 teaspoon chili powder
    Dash garlic powder
3 cups torn lettuce
1 large carrot, shredded
½ cup cherry tomatoes, halved
¼ cup shredded Monterey Jack cheese
¼ cup coarsely crushed taco chips

Crumble pork sausage into a 1-quart casserole. Stir in onion. Micro-cook, uncovered, on 100% power for 3 to 4 minutes or till the meat is no longer pink, stirring once. Drain off fat.

Stir in tomato sauce, canned green chili peppers, flour, chili powder, and garlic powder. Micro-cook, covered, on 100% power for 2 to 3 minutes or till slightly thickened and bubbly.

Meanwhile, in a salad bowl toss together lettuce, carrot, and tomatoes. Top with sausage mixture, cheese, and taco chips. Makes 2 servings.

SCRAMBLED EGGS AND HAM

1 slice boiled ham, cut into strips
    (about 1 ounce)
1 tablespoon sliced green onion
1 tablespoon butter *or* margarine
⅛ teaspoon dried basil, crushed
2 beaten eggs
2 tablespoons milk
2 tablespoons shredded cheddar cheese

In a 15-ounce casserole combine ham, green onion, butter or margarine, and basil. Micro-cook, uncovered, on 100% power for 30 seconds to 1 minute or till mixture is heated through.

Meanwhile, stir together beaten eggs and milk. Pour over ham mixture in casserole. Micro-cook, uncovered, on 50% power for 3 to 3½ minutes or till eggs are nearly set, pushing cooked portions to center of dish several times during cooking. Sprinkle with cheese. Micro-cook, uncovered, on 100% power about 30 seconds more or till the cheese is just melted. Makes 1 serving.

2 slices boiled ham, cut into strips
    (about 2 ounces)
2 tablespoons sliced green onion
1 tablespoon butter *or* margarine
¼ teaspoon dried basil, crushed
4 beaten eggs
¼ cup milk
¼ cup shredded cheddar cheese

In a 7-inch pie plate combine ham, green onion, butter or margarine, and basil. Micro-cook, uncovered, on 100% power for 1 to 1½ minutes or till the mixture is heated through.

Meanwhile, stir together beaten eggs and milk. Pour over ham mixture in pie plate. Micro-cook, uncovered, on 50% power for 4 to 5 minutes or till eggs are nearly set, pushing cooked portions to center of dish several times during cooking. Sprinkle with cheese. Micro-cook, uncovered, on 100% power for 30 seconds to 1 minute more or till the cheese is just melted. Makes 2 servings.

SWEET 'N' SOUR SAUCED PORK

ONE SERVING

¼ pound lean boneless pork
2 teaspoons cooking oil
1 teaspoon sesame oil
1 small carrot, thinly bias sliced
½ of a small green pepper, cut into strips
1 green onion, sliced
2 tablespoons brown sugar
1 teaspoon cornstarch
1 tablespoon water
1 tablespoon red wine vinegar
½ teaspoon soy sauce
  Dash ground ginger
½ of an 8¼-ounce can (about ½ cup) pineapple chunks, drained
  Hot cooked rice

Partially freeze pork. Thinly slice into bite-size strips. Preheat a 6½-inch microwave browning dish on 100% power for 4 minutes. Add cooking oil and sesame oil to browning dish. Swirl to coat the dish. Add the sliced pork. Micro-cook, covered, on 100% power for 1½ to 2½ minutes or till pork is no longer pink, stirring every 30 seconds.

Stir in sliced carrot, green pepper strips, and sliced green onion. Micro-cook, covered, on 100% power for 2 to 3 minutes more or till the vegetables are crisp-tender. Drain off liquid.

In a 2-cup measure stir together the brown sugar and cornstarch. Stir in the water, red wine vinegar, soy sauce, and ground ginger. Micro-cook, uncovered, on 100% power for 1 to 1½ minutes or till thickened and bubbly, stirring every 30 seconds. Stir in drained pineapple chunks. Micro-cook, uncovered, on 100% power about 30 seconds more or till the pineapple is heated through.

Toss the pineapple mixture with the pork mixture. Serve with hot cooked rice. Makes 1 serving.

TWO SERVINGS

½ pound lean boneless pork
4 teaspoons cooking oil
2 teaspoons sesame oil
1 medium carrot, thinly bias sliced
1 small green pepper, cut into strips
2 green onions, sliced
¼ cup packed brown sugar
2 teaspoons cornstarch
2 tablespoons water
2 tablespoons red wine vinegar
1 teaspoon soy sauce
  Dash ground ginger
1 8¼-ounce can (about 1 cup) pineapple chunks, drained
  Hot cooked rice

Partially freeze pork. Thinly slice into bite-size strips. Preheat a 10-inch microwave browning dish on 100% power for 5 minutes. Add cooking oil and sesame oil to browning dish. Swirl to coat the dish. Add the pork. Micro-cook, covered, on 100% power for 2 to 3 minutes or till pork is no longer pink, stirring every minute.

Stir in sliced carrot, green pepper strips, and sliced green onions. Micro-cook, covered, on 100% power for 2 to 4 minutes more or till the vegetables are crisp-tender. Drain off liquid.

In a 2-cup measure stir together the brown sugar and cornstarch. Stir in the water, red wine vinegar, soy sauce, and ground ginger. Micro-cook, uncovered, on 100% power for 1½ to 2½ minutes or till thickened and bubbly, stirring every 30 seconds. Stir in drained pineapple chunks. Micro-cook, uncovered, on 100% power about 45 seconds more or till the pineapple is heated through.

Toss the pineapple mixture with the pork mixture. Serve with hot cooked rice. Makes 2 servings.

SAUSAGE AND CORNBREAD CABBAGE ROLLS

Pictured on pages 14 and 15—

ONE SERVING	TWO SERVINGS
2 large cabbage leaves	4 large cabbage leaves
1 beaten egg	1 beaten egg
1 small apple, chopped (about ½ cup)	1 medium apple, chopped (about 1 cup)
3 tablespoons cornbread stuffing mix	⅓ cup cornbread stuffing mix
1 tablespoon apple juice *or* cider	2 tablespoons apple juice *or* cider
¼ pound bulk pork sausage	½ pound bulk pork sausage
¼ cup water	¼ cup water
3 tablespoons apple juice *or* cider	⅓ cup apple juice *or* cider
½ teaspoon cornstarch	1 teaspoon cornstarch
¼ teaspoon instant beef bouillon granules	½ teaspoon instant beef bouillon granules

Remove center vein of cabbage leaves, keeping each leaf in one piece. Place leaves in a shallow baking dish. Cover with vented clear plastic wrap. Micro-cook, covered, on 100% power for 1 to 3 minutes or till leaves are limp.

Stir together egg, *¼ cup* of the chopped apple, stuffing mix, and 1 tablespoon apple juice or cider. Add sausage; mix well. Divide meat mixture into two equal portions. Place *one* portion of meat mixture on *each* cabbage leaf. Fold in sides. Starting at unfolded edge, roll up each leaf, making sure folded edges are included in roll. Arrange rolls in a shallow baking dish. Pour water over rolls. Cover with vented clear plastic wrap. Micro-cook, covered, on 100% power for 9 to 10 minutes or till the meat is done, rotating the dish a half-turn after 5 minutes. Transfer rolls to a plate. Cover and keep warm.

For sauce, in a 1-cup measure stir together 3 tablespoons apple juice or cider, cornstarch, and instant beef bouillon granules. Stir in the remaining chopped apple. Micro-cook, uncovered, on 100% power for 1½ to 2 minutes or till sauce is thickened and bubbly, stirring every 30 seconds. Spoon sauce atop cabbage rolls. Makes 1 serving.

Remove center vein of cabbage leaves, keeping each leaf in one piece. Place leaves in a shallow baking dish. Cover with vented clear plastic wrap. Micro-cook, covered, on 100% power for 1 to 3 minutes or till leaves are limp.

Stir together egg, *½ cup* of the chopped apple, stuffing mix, and 2 tablespoons apple juice or cider. Add sausage; mix well. Divide meat mixture into four equal portions. Place *one* portion of meat mixture on *each* cabbage leaf. Fold in sides. Starting at unfolded edge, roll up each leaf, making sure folded edges are included in roll. Arrange rolls in a shallow baking dish. Pour water over rolls. Cover with vented clear plastic wrap. Micro-cook, covered, on 100% power for 12 to 14 minutes or till the meat is done, rotating the dish a half-turn after 7 minutes. Transfer rolls to a serving platter. Cover and keep warm.

For sauce, in a 2-cup measure stir together ⅓ cup apple juice or cider, cornstarch, and instant beef bouillon granules. Stir in the remaining chopped apple. Micro-cook, uncovered, on 100% power for 2 to 2½ minutes or till sauce is thickened and bubbly, stirring every 30 seconds. Spoon sauce atop cabbage rolls. Makes 2 servings.

Removing Vein from Cabbage Leaves: To remove the large center vein from the cabbage leaves, use a sharp paring knife to cut along both sides of the vein, keeping the leaf in one piece.

Filling Stuffed Cabbage Leaves: Fill the cabbage leaves by mounding a portion of the meat mixture on each cabbage leaf. Fold in the sides of the cabbage leaf. Starting at an unfolded edge, roll the leaves into individual packets.

SAUSAGE SANDWICHES

ONE SERVING

¼ pound bulk Italian sausage
1 tablespoon chopped onion
2 tablespoons catsup
⅛ teaspoon dried oregano, crushed
1 individual French-style roll, split
1 slice mozzarella cheese

TWO SERVINGS

½ pound bulk Italian sausage
2 tablespoons chopped onion
¼ cup catsup
¼ teaspoon dried oregano, crushed
2 individual French-style rolls, split
2 slices mozzarella cheese

Crumble the Italian sausage into a 20-ounce casserole. Stir in the chopped onion. Micro-cook, uncovered, on 100% power for 2½ to 3½ minutes or till the sausage is done, stirring once. Drain off fat.

Stir in the catsup and oregano. Micro-cook, uncovered, on 100% power for 30 to 45 seconds or till the sausage mixture is heated through. Place the roll bottom on a paper-towel-lined nonmetal plate. Spoon the sausage mixture atop the roll bottom. Top with the slice of cheese and the top of the roll. Micro-cook, uncovered, on 100% power for 30 to 45 seconds more or till cheese is melted. Makes 1 serving.

Crumble the Italian sausage into a 1-quart casserole. Stir in the chopped onion. Micro-cook, uncovered, on 100% power for 3½ to 4½ minutes or till the sausage is done, stirring once. Drain off fat.

Stir in catsup and oregano. Micro-cook, uncovered, on 100% power for 1 to 1½ minutes or till sausage mixture is heated through. Place roll bottoms on a paper-towel-lined nonmetal plate. Spoon some sausage mixture atop each roll bottom. Top each with a slice of cheese and the top of the roll. Micro-cook, uncovered, on 100% power for 45 seconds to 1 minute more or till cheese is melted. Makes 2 servings.

INDIVIDUAL CARROT-PORK LOAVES

ONE SERVING

- 2 tablespoons shredded carrot
- 1 tablespoon chopped onion
- 1 beaten egg yolk
- 2 tablespoons fine dry bread crumbs
   Pinch dried oregano, crushed
- ¼ pound ground pork
- 2 tablespoons shredded cheddar cheese

Micro-cook carrot, onion, and 1 tablespoon *water*, covered, on 100% power about 1 minute or till tender; drain. Stir in egg yolk, bread crumbs, oregano, ⅛ teaspoon salt, and dash *pepper*. Add pork; mix well. Shape into an individual loaf. Place in a shallow baking dish. Micro-cook, loosely covered, on 100% power about 3 minutes or till no longer pink, rotating the dish a quarter-turn and draining off fat every minute. Sprinkle with cheese. Micro-cook, uncovered, on 100% power for 30 to 45 seconds or till cheese is melted. Makes 1 serving.

TWO SERVINGS

- ¼ cup shredded carrot
- 2 tablespoons chopped onion
- 1 beaten egg
- ¼ cup fine dry bread crumbs
- ⅛ teaspoon dried oregano, crushed
- ½ pound ground pork
- ¼ cup shredded cheddar cheese

Micro-cook carrot, onion, and 2 tablespoons *water,* covered, on 100% power about 1½ minutes or till tender; drain. Stir in egg, bread crumbs, oregano, ¼ teaspoon *salt,* and dash *pepper*. Add pork; mix well. Shape into two individual loaves. Place in a shallow baking dish. Micro-cook, loosely covered, on 100% power for 4 to 5 minutes or till no longer pink, giving dish a quarter-turn and draining off fat every 2 minutes. Sprinkle with cheese. Micro-cook, uncovered, on 100% power for 45 seconds to 1½ minutes or till cheese is melted. Makes 2 servings.

ORANGE-GLAZED HAM

ONE SERVING

- 3 ounces fully cooked ham,
   cut into ¾-inch pieces
- 1 stalk celery, bias sliced into
   ½-inch pieces
- ½ of an 11-ounce can mandarin orange
   sections with pineapple
- ½ teaspoon cornstarch
   Dash ground cinnamon

In a 20-ounce casserole micro-cook ham, celery, and 1 tablespoon *water,* covered, on 100% power for 2 to 3 minutes or till heated through. Drain orange sections with pineapple, reserving 3 tablespoons liquid. In a 1-cup measure stir together cornstarch and cinnamon. Stir in reserved liquid. Micro-cook, uncovered, on 100% power for 45 seconds to 1 minute or till thickened and bubbly, stirring twice.

   Drain liquid off ham and celery mixture. Stir in thickened mixture. Stir in orange sections with pineapple. Micro-cook, uncovered, on 100% power for 45 seconds to 1 minute or till heated through. Serve with hot cooked rice, if desired. Makes 1 serving.

TWO SERVINGS

- 6 ounces fully cooked ham,
   cut into ¾-inch pieces
- 2 stalks celery, bias sliced into
   ½-inch pieces
- 1 11-ounce can mandarin orange sections
   with pineapple
- 1 teaspoon cornstarch
- ⅛ teaspoon ground cinnamon

In a 1½-quart casserole micro-cook ham, celery, and 1 tablespoon *water,* covered, on 100% power for 3 to 4 minutes or till heated through. Drain orange sections with pineapple, reserving ⅓ cup liquid. In a 1-cup measure stir together cornstarch and cinnamon. Stir in reserved liquid. Micro-cook, uncovered, on 100% power for 1 to 1½ minutes or till thickened and bubbly, stirring every 30 seconds.

   Drain liquid off ham and celery mixture. Stir in thickened mixture. Stir in orange sections with pineapple. Micro-cook, uncovered, on 100% power about 1½ minutes or till heated through. Serve with hot cooked rice, if desired. Makes 2 servings.

Serve Orange-Glazed
Ham, hot cooked rice,
and spiced tea for lunch
or a light dinner.

LAMB AND PINE NUT STIR-FRY

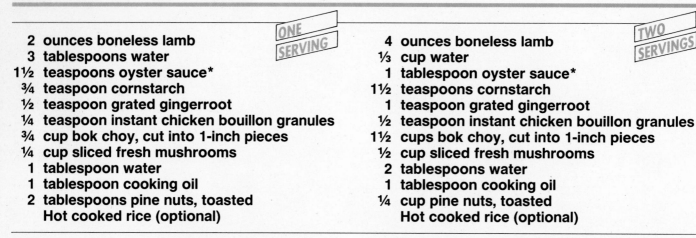

2 ounces boneless lamb	4 ounces boneless lamb
3 tablespoons water	⅓ cup water
1½ teaspoons oyster sauce*	1 tablespoon oyster sauce*
¾ teaspoon cornstarch	1½ teaspoons cornstarch
½ teaspoon grated gingerroot	1 teaspoon grated gingerroot
¼ teaspoon instant chicken bouillon granules	½ teaspoon instant chicken bouillon granules
¾ cup bok choy, cut into 1-inch pieces	1½ cups bok choy, cut into 1-inch pieces
¼ cup sliced fresh mushrooms	½ cup sliced fresh mushrooms
1 tablespoon water	2 tablespoons water
1 tablespoon cooking oil	1 tablespoon cooking oil
2 tablespoons pine nuts, toasted	¼ cup pine nuts, toasted
Hot cooked rice (optional)	Hot cooked rice (optional)

Partially freeze lamb. Thinly slice into bite-size strips. In a 1-cup measure stir together 3 tablespoons water, oyster sauce, cornstarch, grated gingerroot, and chicken bouillon granules. Micro-cook, uncovered, on 100% power for 1 to 1½ minutes or till the mixture is thickened and bubbly, stirring every 30 seconds. Set aside.

In a small nonmetal bowl combine bok choy, sliced mushrooms, and 1 tablespoon water. Cover with vented clear plastic wrap. Micro-cook, covered, on 100% power for 1 to 1½ minutes or till bok choy is just crisp-tender. Drain. Cover and set aside.

Preheat a 6½-inch microwave browning dish on 100% power for 3 minutes. Add cooking oil to browning dish. Swirl to coat dish. Add lamb strips. Micro-cook, covered, on 100% power for 1 to 2 minutes or till lamb is done. Drain off fat. Stir in oyster sauce mixture. Micro-cook, uncovered, on 100% power about 30 seconds or till mixture is heated through. Toss lamb mixture with toasted pine nuts and bok choy mixture. Serve over hot cooked rice, if desired. Makes 1 serving.

*Note: Oyster sauce is an ingredient used frequently in Oriental cooking. You'll find it in either your grocery or an Oriental food store.

Partially freeze lamb. Thinly slice into bite-size strips. In a 2-cup measure stir together ⅓ cup water, oyster sauce, cornstarch, grated gingerroot, and chicken bouillon granules. Micro-cook, uncovered, on 100% power for 1½ to 2 minutes or till thickened and bubbly, stirring every 30 seconds. Set aside.

In a small nonmetal bowl combine bok choy, sliced mushrooms, and 2 tablespoons water. Cover with vented clear plastic wrap. Micro-cook, covered, on 100% power for 3 to 4 minutes or till bok choy is just crisp-tender. Drain. Cover and set aside.

Preheat a 6½-inch microwave browning dish on 100% power for 3 minutes. Add cooking oil to the browning dish. Swirl to coat dish. Add lamb strips. Micro-cook, covered, on 100% power for 1½ to 2½ minutes or till lamb is done. Drain off fat. Stir in oyster sauce mixture. Micro-cook, uncovered, on 100% power about 45 seconds or till mixture is heated through. Toss lamb mixture with toasted pine nuts and bok choy mixture. Serve over hot cooked rice, if desired. Makes 2 servings.

*Note: Oyster sauce is an ingredient used frequently in Oriental cooking. You'll find it in either your grocery or an Oriental food store.

CHUTNEY CHICKEN

¼ cup water
2 tablespoons chopped
   dried apple
2 chicken drumsticks (about 7 ounces total)
2 tablespoons water
½ of an 8-ounce can tomato sauce
   with chopped onion
2 tablespoons raisins
¼ teaspoon cornstarch
¼ teaspoon finely shredded orange peel
   Dash ground cloves
   Dash bottled hot pepper sauce
   Hot cooked rice (optional)

½ cup water
¼ cup chopped dried apple
4 chicken drumsticks
   (about 14 ounces total)
¼ cup water
1 8-ounce can tomato sauce with
   chopped onion
¼ cup raisins
½ teaspoon cornstarch
½ teaspoon finely shredded orange peel
   Dash ground cloves
   Dash bottled hot pepper sauce
   Hot cooked rice (optional)

In a 1-cup measure micro-cook the ¼ cup water, uncovered, on 100% power for 45 seconds to 1 minute or till boiling. Stir in dried apple. Let stand for 5 minutes. Drain off excess water.

Meanwhile, place chicken drumsticks in a shallow baking dish. Pour the 2 tablespoons water over the drumsticks. Cover with vented clear plastic wrap. Micro-cook, covered, on 100% power for 3 to 4 minutes or till chicken is tender, rotating the dish a quarter-turn every minute. Drain off liquid. Transfer chicken drumsticks to a plate. Cover and keep warm while preparing tomato sauce.

For tomato sauce, in a 2-cup measure combine tomato sauce with chopped onion, raisins, cornstarch, shredded orange peel, ground cloves, bottled hot pepper sauce, and drained apple. Micro-cook, uncovered, on 100% power for 1½ to 2½ minutes or till thickened and bubbly, stirring every 30 seconds. Spoon over chicken drumsticks. If desired, serve with hot cooked rice. Makes 1 serving.

In a 2-cup measure micro-cook the ½ cup water, uncovered, on 100% power for 1 to 2 minutes or till boiling. Stir in dried apple. Let stand for 5 minutes. Drain off excess water.

Meanwhile, place chicken drumsticks in a shallow baking dish. Pour the ¼ cup water over the drumsticks. Cover with vented clear plastic wrap. Micro-cook, covered, on 100% power for 5 to 6 minutes or till the chicken is tender, rotating the dish a quarter-turn every minute. Drain off liquid. Transfer chicken drumsticks to a serving platter. Cover and keep warm while preparing tomato sauce.

For tomato sauce, in a 4-cup measure combine tomato sauce with chopped onion, raisins, cornstarch, shredded orange peel, ground cloves, bottled hot pepper sauce, and drained apple. Micro-cook, uncovered, on 100% power for 2½ to 3½ minutes or till thickened and bubbly, stirring every minute. Spoon over chicken drumsticks. If desired, serve with hot cooked rice. Makes 2 servings.

ORANGE CHICKEN

ONE SERVING

½ of a whole large chicken breast, skinned and boned
¼ cup cooked rice
⅛ teaspoon finely shredded orange peel
Dash ground cinnamon
¼ cup orange juice
¾ teaspoon cornstarch
1 tablespoon broken walnuts
Cucumber rose (optional)

TWO SERVINGS

1 whole large chicken breast, skinned and boned
½ cup cooked rice
¼ teaspoon finely shredded orange peel
Dash ground cinnamon
½ cup orange juice
1½ teaspoons cornstarch
2 tablespoons broken walnuts
Cucumber rose (optional)

Place chicken, boned side up, between two pieces of clear plastic wrap. Working from the center to the edges, pound lightly with a meat mallet, forming a rectangle about ⅛ inch thick. Remove plastic wrap. Sprinkle chicken with salt.

In a small bowl stir together cooked rice, shredded orange peel, and ground cinnamon. Spoon the rice-orange peel mixture atop the chicken breast portion, spreading it to within ¼ inch of the edges. Fold in sides of the chicken breast portion; roll up jelly-roll style, starting with one end.

Place chicken roll, seam side down, in a shallow baking dish. Cover with vented clear plastic wrap. Micro-cook the chicken roll, covered, on 50% power for 4 to 5 minutes or till the chicken is tender, rotating the dish a half-turn after 2 minutes. Transfer chicken roll to a plate.

For orange sauce, in a 1-cup measure stir together orange juice and cornstarch. Micro-cook, uncovered, on 100% power about 1 minute or till the orange juice mixture is thickened and bubbly, stirring every 20 seconds. Stir in broken walnuts. Spoon the orange sauce atop the chicken roll on the plate. Garnish with cucumber rose, if desired. Makes 1 serving.

Halve chicken breast lengthwise. Place one portion, boned side up, between two pieces of clear plastic wrap. Working from the center to the edges, pound lightly with a meat mallet, forming a rectangle about ⅛ inch thick. Remove plastic wrap. Sprinkle chicken with salt. Repeat with the remaining portion of chicken.

In a small bowl stir together cooked rice, shredded orange peel, and ground cinnamon. Spoon half of the rice-orange peel mixture atop one chicken breast portion, spreading it to within ¼ inch of the edges. Fold in sides; roll up jelly-roll style, starting with one end. Repeat with remaining rice-orange peel mixture and chicken portion.

Place chicken rolls, seam side down, in a shallow baking dish. Cover with vented clear plastic wrap. Micro-cook the chicken rolls, covered, on 50% power for 7 to 8 minutes or till chicken is tender, rotating the dish a half-turn after 4 minutes. Transfer chicken rolls to a serving platter.

For orange sauce, in a 1-cup measure stir together orange juice and cornstarch. Micro-cook, uncovered, on 100% power for 1½ to 2 minutes or till the mixture is thickened and bubbly, stirring every 20 seconds. Stir in broken walnuts. Spoon the orange sauce atop the chicken rolls on the serving platter. Garnish with a cucumber rose, if desired. Makes 2 servings.

CITRUS-BUTTERED LOBSTER TAILS

ONE SERVING

- 1 8-ounce frozen lobster tail
- ¼ cup water
- 2 tablespoons butter *or* margarine
- 1½ teaspoons lemon juice
- ¼ teaspoon finely shredded orange peel
  Dash salt
  Dash ground ginger
  Dash paprika

TWO SERVINGS

- 2 8-ounce frozen lobster tails
- ½ cup water
- ¼ cup butter *or* margarine
- 1 tablespoon lemon juice
- ½ teaspoon finely shredded orange peel
- ⅛ teaspoon salt
  Dash ground ginger
  Dash paprika

Place lobster tail in a shallow baking dish. Micro-cook, covered, on 30% power about 5 minutes or till thawed, rotating dish a quarter-turn once. The tail is thawed when the shell is flexible enough to bend. Using a heavy knife, cut through the center of the top shell. Continue cutting through meat, but not through undershell. Spread tail open, butterfly-style, so meat is on top. Return to shallow baking dish. Pour water atop. Micro-cook, covered, on 50% power for 5 to 7 minutes or just till meat is opaque, rotating dish a quarter-turn every minute. (Shield cooked meat with small pieces of foil, if necessary, to prevent overcooking.) Let stand, covered, for 5 minutes.

Meanwhile, combine butter or margarine, lemon juice, orange peel, salt, ginger, and paprika. Micro-cook, uncovered, on 100% power for 30 to 45 seconds or till butter is melted. Mix well. Drizzle lobster tail with butter mixture. Makes 1 serving.

Place lobster tails in a shallow baking dish. Micro-cook, covered, on 30% power for 7 to 8 minutes or till thawed, rotating dish a quarter-turn once. The tails are thawed when the shells are flexible enough to bend. Using a heavy knife, cut through the center of the top shells. Continue cutting through meat, but not through undershells. Spread tails open, butterfly-style, so meat is on top. Return to shallow baking dish. Pour water atop. Micro-cook, covered, on 50% power for 6 to 8 minutes or just till meat is opaque, rotating dish a quarter-turn every minute. (Shield cooked meat with small pieces of foil, if necessary, to prevent overcooking.) Let stand, covered, for 5 minutes.

Meanwhile, combine butter or margarine, lemon juice, orange peel, salt, ginger, and paprika. Micro-cook, uncovered, on 100% power for 1½ to 2½ minutes or till butter is melted. Mix well. Drizzle lobster tails with butter mixture. Makes 2 servings.

Thawing Lobster Tails: Determine if a lobster tail is thawed by gently bending it. If the tail is flexible enough to bend, it is thawed. If the tail is not flexible, micro-cook it for a few seconds more on 30% power.

Serving Lobster Tails: Before serving the butterflied lobster tails, transfer each lobster tail to a serving platter or plate and spoon the citrus butter mixture over the cooked meat inside the shell.

Salmon Steaks with Wine
Sauce is perfect for a
special dinner entrée (see
recipe, page 34).

SALMON STEAKS WITH WINE SAUCE

Pictured on pages 32 and 33—

ONE SERVING			**TWO SERVINGS**	

1	4-ounce fresh *or* frozen salmon steak		2	4-ounce fresh *or* frozen salmon steaks
1	teaspoon cooking oil		2	teaspoons cooking oil
1½	teaspoons butter *or* margarine		1	tablespoon butter *or* margarine
¼	teaspoon cornstarch		1	teaspoon cornstarch
	Dash white pepper			Dash white pepper
¼	cup light cream		½	cup light cream
1	beaten egg yolk		1	beaten egg yolk
1	tablespoon dry white wine		2	tablespoons dry white wine
	Seedless green grapes (optional)			Seedless green grapes (optional)

Thaw salmon steak, if frozen. Preheat a 6½-inch microwave browning dish on 100% power for 3 minutes. Add cooking oil to the browning dish; swirl to coat the dish. Place fresh or thawed salmon steak in the browning dish. Micro-cook, covered, on 100% power for 30 seconds. Turn the salmon steak and micro-cook, covered, on 50% power for 1 to 1½ minutes or till the salmon flakes easily when tested with a fork. Let the salmon steak stand, covered, while preparing the wine sauce.

For wine sauce, in a 2-cup measure micro-cook the butter or margarine, uncovered, on 100% power for 30 to 45 seconds or till melted. Stir in cornstarch and white pepper. Stir in light cream. Micro-cook, uncovered, on 100% power for 1 to 2 minutes or till the cream mixture is thickened and bubbly, stirring once. Stir *half* of the hot cream mixture into the beaten egg yolk. Return all to the 2-cup measure. Micro-cook, uncovered, on 50% power for 30 seconds, stirring once. Stir till mixture is smooth. Stir in dry white wine.

Transfer the salmon steak to a plate. Spoon the wine sauce atop. Garnish with seedless green grapes, if desired. Makes 1 serving.

Thaw salmon steaks, if frozen. Preheat a 6½-inch microwave browning dish on 100% power for 3 minutes. Add cooking oil to the browning dish; swirl to coat the dish. Place fresh or thawed salmon steaks in the browning dish. Micro-cook, covered, on 100% power for 30 seconds. Turn the salmon steaks and micro-cook, covered, on 50% power about 3 minutes or till the salmon flakes easily when tested with a fork. Let the salmon steaks stand, covered, while preparing the wine sauce.

For the wine sauce, in a 4-cup measure micro-cook the butter or margarine, uncovered, on 100% power for 45 seconds to 1 minute or till melted. Stir in the cornstarch and white pepper. Stir in light cream. Micro-cook, uncovered, on 100% power for 2 to 3 minutes or till the cream mixture is thickened and bubbly, stirring every minute. Stir *half* of the hot cream mixture into the beaten egg yolk. Return all to the 4-cup measure. Micro-cook, uncovered, on 50% power for 1 minute, stirring every 15 seconds. Stir till mixture is smooth. Stir in dry white wine.

Transfer the salmon steaks to a serving platter. Spoon the wine sauce atop. Garnish with seedless green grapes, if desired. Makes 2 servings.

CRAB-TOPPED SHRIMP

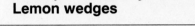

One Serving	Two Servings

6 fresh *or* frozen large shrimp in shells
1 tablespoon sliced green onion
1 tablespoon butter *or* margarine
½ teaspoon lemon juice
   Dash bottled hot pepper sauce
½ of a 5½-ounce can crab meat, drained, flaked, and cartilage removed
1 tablespoon fine dry bread crumbs
   Lemon wedges

Thaw large shrimp, if frozen. To shell fresh or thawed shrimp, open each shell lengthwise down the body. Hold the shrimp in one hand and carefully peel back the shell starting with the head end. Gently pull on the tail portion of the shell to remove the entire shell. Butterfly shrimp by cutting down the back almost but not all the way through; remove vein. Repeat with the remaining shrimp. Set aside.

In a small nonmetal bowl micro-cook sliced green onion and butter or margarine, uncovered, on 100% power for 1 to 1½ minutes or till the green onion is tender. Stir in lemon juice and bottled hot pepper sauce. Toss with the flaked crab meat and fine dry bread crumbs.

Spread shrimp open. Place, cut side up, in a 10-ounce oval casserole. Cover with vented clear plastic wrap. Micro-cook, covered, on 100% power for 45 seconds, rotating the casserole a half-turn once. Drain off liquid and rearrange shrimp, placing the least-cooked portions to the outside of the casserole.

Spoon crab mixture over shrimp. Micro-cook, covered, on 100% power about 1½ minutes or till shrimp are done and crab mixture is heated through, rotating the casserole a half-turn once. Serve with lemon wedges. Makes 1 serving.

12 fresh *or* frozen large shrimp in shells
2 tablespoons sliced green onion
1 tablespoon butter *or* margarine
1 teaspoon lemon juice
   Dash bottled hot pepper sauce
1 5½-ounce can crab meat, drained, flaked, and cartilage removed
2 tablespoons fine dry bread crumbs
   Lemon wedges

Thaw large shrimp, if frozen. To shell fresh or thawed shrimp, open each shell lengthwise down the body. Hold the shrimp in one hand and carefully peel back the shell starting with the head end. Gently pull on the tail portion of the shell to remove the entire shell. Butterfly shrimp by cutting down the back almost but not all the way through; remove vein. Repeat with remaining shrimp. Set aside.

In a small nonmetal bowl micro-cook sliced green onion and the butter or margarine, uncovered, on 100% power for 1½ to 2 minutes or till the green onion is tender. Stir in lemon juice and bottled hot pepper sauce. Toss with the flaked crab meat and fine dry bread crumbs.

Spread shrimp open. Place, cut side up, in two 10-ounce oval casseroles. Cover with vented clear plastic wrap. Micro-cook, covered, on 100% power for 1½ minutes, rotating the casseroles a half-turn once. Drain off liquid and rearrange shrimp, placing the least-cooked portions to the outside of the casseroles.

Spoon crab mixture over shrimp. Micro-cook, covered, on 100% power about 2½ minutes or till shrimp are done and crab mixture is heated through, rotating the casseroles a half-turn once. Serve with lemon wedges. Makes 2 servings.

TOASTY WALNUT MUFFINS

ONE SERVING

- 2 tablespoons quick-cooking rolled oats
- ¼ cup all-purpose flour
- 1 tablespoon sugar
- ¼ teaspoon baking powder
  Dash ground cinnamon
- 1 beaten egg yolk
- 1 tablespoon cooking oil
- 1 tablespoon milk
- 2 tablespoons broken walnuts, toasted
- 1 tablespoon raisins
- 1 teaspoon all-purpose flour
- ½ teaspoon brown sugar
- ½ teaspoon butter *or* margarine

TWO SERVINGS

- ¼ cup quick-cooking rolled oats
- ½ cup all-purpose flour
- 2 tablespoons sugar
- ½ teaspoon baking powder
  Dash ground cinnamon
- 1 beaten egg yolk
- 2 tablespoons cooking oil
- 2 tablespoons milk
- ¼ cup broken walnuts, toasted
- 2 tablespoons raisins
- 2 teaspoons all-purpose flour
- 1 teaspoon brown sugar
- 1 teaspoon butter *or* margarine

Stir together oats and 1 tablespoon warm *water*; let stand for 5 minutes. Meanwhile, stir together ¼ cup flour, sugar, baking powder, cinnamon, and dash *salt*. Stir egg yolk, oil, and milk into oat mixture; add to dry ingredients, stirring just till moistened. Fold in *5 teaspoons* of the walnuts and the raisins.

Line two 6-ounce custard cups with paper bake cups. Fill ⅔ full. Combine 1 teaspoon flour, brown sugar, butter, and remaining walnuts. Sprinkle atop muffins. Micro-cook, uncovered, on 100% power for 1 to 1½ minutes or till done, rearranging once. (When done, surface may still appear moist, but a wooden pick inserted near the center should come out clean.) Remove from custard cups. Let stand on a wire rack for 5 minutes. Serve warm. Makes 2 muffins.

Stir together oats and 2 tablespoons warm *water*; let stand for 5 minutes. Meanwhile, stir together ½ cup flour, sugar, baking powder, cinnamon, and dash *salt*. Stir egg yolk, oil, and milk into oat mixture; add to dry ingredients, stirring just till moistened. Fold in *3 tablespoons* of the walnuts and the raisins.

Line four 6-ounce custard cups with paper bake cups. Fill ⅔ full. Combine 2 teaspoons flour, brown sugar, butter, and remaining walnuts. Sprinkle atop muffins. Micro-cook, uncovered, on 100% power for 1½ to 2½ minutes or till done, rearranging twice. (When done, surface may still appear moist, but a wooden pick inserted near the center should come out clean.) Remove from custard cups. Let stand on a wire rack for 5 minutes. Serve warm. Makes 4 muffins.

Testing Muffins for Doneness: When done, the surface may still appear moist, but a wooden pick inserted near the center should come out clean.

CORN MUFFINS

3 tablespoons all-purpose flour
3 tablespoons yellow cornmeal
1 tablespoon sugar
¾ teaspoon baking powder
⅛ teaspoon salt
1 beaten egg yolk
2 tablespoons milk
2 teaspoons cooking oil
  Yellow cornmeal

⅓ cup all-purpose flour
⅓ cup yellow cornmeal
2 tablespoons sugar
1½ teaspoons baking powder
¼ teaspoon salt
1 beaten egg
¼ cup milk
4 teaspoons cooking oil
  Yellow cornmeal

In a small bowl stir together flour, 3 tablespoons yellow cornmeal, sugar, baking powder, and salt. Make a well in the center of the dry ingredients. Stir together beaten egg yolk, milk, and cooking oil. Add all at once to the dry ingredients, stirring just till moistened. Line two 6-ounce custard cups with paper bake cups. Fill cups ⅔ full. Sprinkle a little additional cornmeal atop muffins. Micro-cook, uncovered, on 100% power about 45 seconds or till done, rearranging once. (When done, surface may appear moist, but a wooden pick inserted near the center should come out clean.) Makes 2 muffins.

In a small bowl stir together flour, ⅓ cup yellow cornmeal, sugar, baking powder, and salt. Make a well in the center of the dry ingredients. Stir together beaten egg, milk, and cooking oil. Add all at once to the dry ingredients, stirring just till moistened. Line four 6-ounce custard cups with paper bake cups. Fill the cups ⅔ full. Sprinkle a little additional cornmeal atop muffins. Micro-cook, uncovered, on 100% power about 1½ minutes or till done, rearranging twice. (When done, the surface may appear moist, but a wooden pick inserted near the center should come out clean.) Makes 4 muffins.

RICE PILAF

¼ cup sliced fresh mushrooms
1 green onion, sliced
1½ teaspoons butter *or* margarine
⅔ cup water*
3 tablespoons long grain rice
⅛ of a medium sweet red *or* green pepper,
  cut into 1-inch julienne strips
⅛ teaspoon salt
⅛ teaspoon dried sage, crushed
1 teaspoon snipped parsley

½ cup sliced fresh mushrooms
2 green onions, sliced
1 tablespoon butter *or* margarine
⅔ cup water*
⅓ cup long grain rice
¼ of a medium sweet red *or* green pepper,
  cut into 1-inch julienne strips
¼ teaspoon salt
¼ teaspoon dried sage, crushed
2 teaspoons snipped parsley

In a 1-quart casserole micro-cook mushrooms, onion, and butter or margarine, uncovered, on 100% power for 1 to 2 minutes or till vegetables are tender. Stir in water, rice, red or green pepper, salt, and sage. Micro-cook, covered, on 100% power for 2 to 3 minutes or till boiling. Micro-cook, covered, on 50% power for 12 to 15 minutes or till rice is tender and liquid is absorbed, stirring once. Stir in parsley. Let stand, covered, for 5 minutes. Makes 1 serving.

Note: Because of the rate at which water evaporates during cooking, both the one- and two-serving versions use ⅔ cup water.

In a 1-quart casserole micro-cook mushrooms, onion, and butter or margarine, uncovered, on 100% power for 1½ to 2½ minutes or till vegetables are tender. Stir in water, rice, red or green pepper, salt, and sage. Micro-cook, covered, on 100% power for 2 to 3 minutes or till boiling. Micro-cook, covered, on 50% power for 14 to 16 minutes or till rice is tender and liquid is absorbed, stirring once. Stir in parsley. Let stand, covered, for 5 minutes. Makes 2 servings.

HERBED TOMATO SOUP

ONE SERVING	TWO SERVINGS
1 tablespoon chopped onion 1½ teaspoons butter *or* margarine ½ of an 8-ounce can (½ cup) tomato sauce ⅛ teaspoon dried basil, crushed Pinch dried thyme, crushed Dash pepper ½ cup water ½ teaspoon instant chicken bouillon granules Parmesan Croutons (see recipe below)	2 tablespoons chopped onion 1 tablespoon butter *or* margarine 1 8-ounce can (1 cup) tomato sauce ¼ teaspoon dried basil, crushed ⅛ teaspoon dried thyme, crushed Dash pepper 1 cup water 1 teaspoon instant chicken bouillon granules Parmesan Croutons (see recipe below)

In a 2-cup measure micro-cook onion and butter or margarine, uncovered, on 100% power for 30 seconds to 1 minute or till the onion is tender but not brown. Stir in the tomato sauce, dried basil, dried thyme, and pepper. Micro-cook, uncovered, on 50% power for 2 to 3 minutes or just till boiling. Stir in the water and instant chicken bouillon granules. Micro-cook, uncovered, on 100% power for 1 to 1½ minutes or till the mixture is heated through. Serve with Parmesan Croutons. Makes 1 serving.

In a 4-cup measure micro-cook onion and butter or margarine, uncovered, on 100% power for 1 to 1½ minutes or till the onion is tender but not brown. Stir in the tomato sauce, dried basil, dried thyme, and pepper. Micro-cook, uncovered, on 50% power for 4 to 5 minutes or just till boiling. Stir in the water and instant chicken bouillon granules. Micro-cook, uncovered, on 100% power for 2 to 3 minutes or till the mixture is heated through. Serve with the Parmesan Croutons. Makes 2 servings.

PARMESAN CROUTONS

ONE SERVING	TWO SERVINGS
½ slice whole wheat bread 1½ teaspoons butter *or* margarine 1½ teaspoons grated Parmesan cheese	1 slice whole wheat bread 1 tablespoon butter *or* margarine 1 tablespoon grated Parmesan cheese

Trim crust from bread. Cut the half-slice of bread into halves, making squares. Diagonally cut each square into halves, making triangles. Arrange the bread triangles in a shallow baking dish or pie plate. Micro-cook, uncovered, on 100% power for 30 seconds to 1 minute or till the bread is dry. Remove the bread triangles from the microwave oven.

In a custard cup micro-cook butter or margarine, uncovered, on 100% power for 30 to 40 seconds or till melted. Drizzle over bread triangles. Sprinkle with Parmesan cheese. Makes 4 croutons.

Trim crust from bread. Cut bread slice into quarters, making squares. Diagonally cut each square into halves, making triangles. Arrange bread triangles in a shallow baking dish or pie plate. Micro-cook, uncovered, on 100% power for 1 to 1½ minutes or till bread is dry. Remove the bread from the microwave oven.

In a custard cup micro-cook butter or margarine, uncovered, on 100% power for 40 to 50 seconds or till melted. Drizzle over bread triangles. Sprinkle with Parmesan cheese. Makes 8 croutons.

CREAMY MUSHROOM SOUP

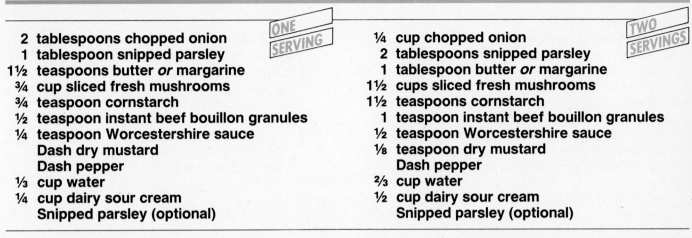

ONE SERVING	TWO SERVINGS
2 **tablespoons chopped onion**	¼ **cup chopped onion**
1 **tablespoon snipped parsley**	2 **tablespoons snipped parsley**
1½ **teaspoons butter or margarine**	1 **tablespoon butter or margarine**
¾ **cup sliced fresh mushrooms**	1½ **cups sliced fresh mushrooms**
¾ **teaspoon cornstarch**	1½ **teaspoons cornstarch**
½ **teaspoon instant beef bouillon granules**	1 **teaspoon instant beef bouillon granules**
¼ **teaspoon Worcestershire sauce**	½ **teaspoon Worcestershire sauce**
Dash dry mustard	⅛ **teaspoon dry mustard**
Dash pepper	**Dash pepper**
⅓ **cup water**	⅔ **cup water**
¼ **cup dairy sour cream**	½ **cup dairy sour cream**
Snipped parsley (optional)	**Snipped parsley (optional)**

In a 2-cup measure micro-cook the chopped onion, the 1 tablespoon snipped parsley, and butter or margarine, uncovered, on 100% power for 30 seconds to 1 minute or till the onion is tender but not brown. Stir in the sliced fresh mushrooms. Micro-cook, covered, on 100% power for 1½ to 2 minutes or till the mushrooms are tender, stirring once.

Stir in cornstarch, instant beef bouillon granules, Worcestershire sauce, dry mustard, and pepper. Add water; mix well. Micro-cook, uncovered, on 100% power for 1½ to 2 minutes or till the mushroom mixture is thickened and bubbly, stirring once.

Combine hot mushroom mixture and dairy sour cream in a blender container. Cover and blend till mixture is nearly smooth. Pour back into the 2-cup measure. Micro-cook, uncovered, on 100% power for 45 seconds to 1 minute or till the mushroom mixture is heated through. *Do not* boil. Garnish with additional snipped parsley, if desired. Makes 1 serving.

In a 4-cup measure micro-cook the chopped onion, the 2 tablespoons snipped parsley, and butter or margarine, uncovered, on 100% power for 1 to 1½ minutes or till the onion is tender but not brown. Stir in the sliced fresh mushrooms. Micro-cook, covered, on 100% power for 2 to 3 minutes or till the mushrooms are tender, stirring once.

Stir in cornstarch, beef bouillon granules, Worcestershire sauce, dry mustard, and pepper. Add water; mix well. Micro-cook, uncovered, on 100% power for 3 to 4 minutes or till the mushroom mixture is thickened and bubbly, stirring twice.

Combine hot mushroom mixture and dairy sour cream in a blender container. Cover and blend till the mixture is nearly smooth. Pour back into the 4-cup measure. Micro-cook, uncovered, on 100% power about 1 minute or till the mushroom mixture is heated through. *Do not* boil. Garnish with additional snipped parsley, if desired. Makes 2 servings.

Washing Your Blender: After making Creamy Mushroom Soup, use this quick clean-up method to wash your blender. Simply fill the blender container about ⅓ full with lukewarm water and add a small amount of detergent. Replace the lid and run the motor a few seconds or till the blender container is clean. Rinse, dry, and return the blender container to its base.

FRUIT SOUP

ONE SERVING

- ⅓ cup apricot nectar
- ½ teaspoon cornstarch
- 1½ teaspoons brandy
- 1½ teaspoons honey
  Dash ground allspice
- ½ cup peeled and sliced papayas, peaches, *or* pineapple; cut-up apricots, nectarines, *or* plums; *or* halved and pitted dark sweet cherries

In a small nonmetal bowl stir together apricot nectar and cornstarch. Stir in brandy, honey, and allspice. Micro-cook, uncovered, on 100% power for 1 to 2 minutes or till thickened and bubbly, stirring every 30 seconds. Stir in fruit. Micro-cook, uncovered, on 100% power for 30 to 45 seconds or till heated through. Chill thoroughly, if desired. Serve hot or cold. Makes 1 serving.

TWO SERVINGS

- ⅔ cup apricot nectar
- 1 teaspoon cornstarch
- 1 tablespoon brandy
- 1 tablespoon honey
- ⅛ teaspoon ground allspice
- 1 cup peeled and sliced papayas, peaches, *or* pineapple; cut-up apricots, nectarines, *or* plums; *or* halved and pitted dark sweet cherries

In a nonmetal bowl stir together apricot nectar and cornstarch. Stir in brandy, honey, and allspice. Micro-cook, uncovered, on 100% power for 2 to 3 minutes or till the mixture is thickened and bubbly, stirring every 30 seconds. Stir in fruit. Micro-cook, uncovered, on 100% power for 45 seconds to 1 minute or till heated through. Chill thoroughly, if desired. Serve hot or cold. Makes 2 servings.

ORIENTAL PEA PODS AND CARROTS

ONE SERVING

- 2 tablespoons water
- 1½ teaspoons soy sauce
- ½ teaspoon cornstarch
  Dash crushed red pepper
- 1 small carrot, thinly bias sliced
- 1 teaspoon water
- ¼ of a 6-ounce package frozen pea pods
- 1 tablespoon broken walnuts
- 1 teaspoon butter *or* margarine

In a custard cup stir together 2 tablespoons water, soy sauce, cornstarch, and crushed red pepper. Micro-cook, uncovered, on 100% power for 30 seconds to 1 minute or till thickened and bubbly, stirring once.

Place the carrot in a 10-ounce casserole. Sprinkle with 1 teaspoon water. Micro-cook, covered, on 100% power for 2 minutes. Drain. Toss together carrot, pea pods, and walnuts; add butter or margarine. Micro-cook, covered, on 100% power about 1 minute or till the vegetables are crisp-tender. Toss with the soy sauce mixture. Makes 1 serving.

TWO SERVINGS

- ¼ cup water
- 1 tablespoon soy sauce
- 1 teaspoon cornstarch
  Dash crushed red pepper
- 1 medium carrot, thinly bias sliced
- 2 teaspoons water
- ½ of a 6-ounce package frozen pea pods
- 2 tablespoons broken walnuts
- 1 teaspoon butter *or* margarine

In a custard cup stir together ¼ cup water, soy sauce, cornstarch, and crushed red pepper. Micro-cook, uncovered, on 100% power for 1 to 1½ minutes or till thickened and bubbly, stirring every 30 seconds.

Place the carrot in a 20-ounce casserole. Sprinkle with 2 teaspoons water. Micro-cook, covered, on 100% power for 2½ minutes. Drain. Toss together carrot, pea pods, and walnuts; add butter or margarine. Micro-cook, covered, on 100% power about 1½ minutes or till the vegetables are crisp-tender. Toss with the soy sauce mixture. Makes 2 servings.

•
Oriental Pea Pods and Carrots can be a healthy snack after tennis or a delicious side dish with lunch or dinner.

CARROTS IN ORANGE-BASIL BUTTER

Pictured on pages 14 and 15—

ONE SERVING

- 1 **medium carrot, cut into**
    julienne strips
- 1 **tablespoon water**
- 1 **teaspoon butter** *or* **margarine**
    Pinch finely shredded orange peel
    Pinch dried basil, crushed
    Snipped parsley (optional)

Place the carrot strips in a 10-ounce casserole. Sprinkle with water. Micro-cook, covered, on 100% power for 1 to 1½ minutes or just till the carrot strips are crisp-tender. Let stand, covered, while preparing butter mixture.

For butter mixture, in a custard cup combine butter or margarine, orange peel, and basil. Micro-cook, uncovered, on 100% power for 15 to 30 seconds or till the butter or margarine is melted. Drain carrot strips. Drizzle butter mixture over carrot strips. Garnish with snipped parsley, if desired. Makes 1 serving.

TWO SERVINGS

- 2 **medium carrots, cut into**
    julienne strips
- 1 **tablespoon water**
- 1 **tablespoon butter** *or* **margarine**
- ⅛ **teaspoon finely shredded orange peel**
    Pinch dried basil, crushed
    Snipped parsley (optional)

Place carrot strips in a 1-quart casserole. Sprinkle with water. Micro-cook, covered, on 100% power for 2 to 3 minutes or just till carrot strips are crisp-tender. Let stand, covered, while preparing butter mixture.

For butter mixture, in a custard cup combine butter or margarine, orange peel, and basil. Micro-cook, uncovered, on 100% power about 30 seconds or till the butter or margarine is melted. Drain carrots. Drizzle butter mixture over carrot strips. Garnish with snipped parsley, if desired. Makes 2 servings.

ORANGE AND PEANUT SWEET POTATOES

ONE SERVING

- 1 **medium sweet potato**
- ⅛ **teaspoon finely shredded**
    orange peel (set aside)
- 1 **tablespoon orange juice**
- ¼ **cup orange juice**
- ¾ **teaspoon cornstarch**
- 2 **teaspoons honey** *or* **maple-flavored syrup**
- 1 **tablespoon peanuts**

Peel and slice sweet potato crosswise into ½-inch-thick slices. Place in a 10-ounce casserole. Sprinkle lightly with salt. Sprinkle with 1 tablespoon orange juice. Micro-cook, covered, on 100% power for 4 to 6 minutes or till potato is tender. Let stand, covered, while preparing sauce.

For sauce, in a 1-cup measure stir together ¼ cup orange juice, cornstarch, and shredded orange peel. Stir in honey or maple-flavored syrup. Micro-cook, uncovered, on 100% power for 30 seconds to 1 minute or till thickened and bubbly, stirring every 15 seconds. Stir together sauce and potato slices. Sprinkle with peanuts. Makes 1 serving.

TWO SERVINGS

- 2 **medium sweet potatoes**
- ¼ **teaspoon finely shredded**
    orange peel (set side)
- 2 **tablespoons orange juice**
- ½ **cup orange juice**
- 2 **teaspoons cornstarch**
- 4 **teaspoons honey** *or* **maple-flavored syrup**
- 2 **tablespoons peanuts**

Peel and slice sweet potatoes crosswise into ½-inch-thick slices. Place in a 1-quart casserole. Sprinkle lightly with salt. Sprinkle with 2 tablespoons orange juice. Micro-cook, covered, on 100% power for 6 to 8 minutes or till potatoes are tender. Let stand, covered, while preparing sauce.

For sauce, in a 2-cup measure stir together ½ cup orange juice, cornstarch, and finely shredded orange peel. Stir in honey or maple-flavored syrup. Micro-cook, uncovered, on 100% power for 1 to 2 minutes or till thickened and bubbly, stirring every 30 seconds. Stir together sauce and potato slices. Sprinkle with peanuts. Makes 2 servings.

TWICE-BAKED POTATOES

ONE SERVING

1 **medium baking potato**
2 **tablespoons shredded cheddar cheese (½ ounce)**
1½ **teaspoons butter *or* margarine**
1 **teaspoon sliced green onion**
1 **to 2 tablespoons milk**
  Paprika (optional)

TWO SERVINGS

2 **medium baking potatoes**
¼ **cup shredded cheddar cheese (1 ounce)**
1 **tablespoon butter *or* margarine**
2 **teaspoons sliced green onion**
2 **to 4 tablespoons milk**
  Paprika (optional)

Scrub baking potato with a brush. Prick with a fork in several places. Place potato in a shallow baking dish. Micro-cook, uncovered, on 100% power for 4 to 5 minutes or till potato is tender. Cut a lengthwise slice from the top of the potato. Discard the skin from the lengthwise slice; place the potato portion from the lengthwise slice in a mixing bowl.

Scoop out the insides of the potato, leaving a ¼-inch-thick shell; reserve the shell. Add the insides of the potato to the mixing bowl containing the potato portion from the top slice; mash. Stir in shredded cheddar cheese, butter or margarine, and sliced green onion. Beat in enough milk to give the mixture a stiff consistency. Season to taste with salt and pepper.

Pile the mashed potato mixture into the reserved potato shell. Return to the shallow baking dish. Micro-cook, uncovered, on 100% power for 1 to 2 minutes or till potato mixture is heated through. Sprinkle with paprika, if desired. Makes 1 serving.

Scrub baking potatoes with a brush. Prick with a fork in several places. Place potatoes in a shallow baking dish. Micro-cook, uncovered, on 100% power for 6 to 8 minutes or till potatoes are tender. Cut a lengthwise slice from the top of each potato. Discard the skin from the lengthwise slices; place the potato portions from the lengthwise slices in a mixing bowl.

Scoop out the insides of the potatoes, leaving two ¼-inch-thick shells; reserve the shells. Add the insides of the potatoes to the mixing bowl containing the potato portions from the top slices; mash. Stir in shredded cheddar cheese, butter or margarine, and sliced green onion. Beat in enough milk to give the mixture a stiff consistency. Season to taste with salt and pepper.

Pile the mashed potato mixture into the reserved potato shells. Return to the shallow baking dish. Micro-cook, uncovered, on 100% power for 2 to 3 minutes or till potato mixture is heated through. Sprinkle with paprika, if desired. Makes 2 servings.

Selecting Potatoes for Twice-Baked Potatoes:
Potato varieties range in shape from oblong to round and in skin color from creamy white to red and russet brown. Although there are some all-purpose varieties of potatoes, many are best suited to a specific use. For recipes such as Twice-Baked Potatoes, select long, oval, russet brown, baking potatoes. They have a mealy interior and give you the best results for this type of potato dish.

RICE-STUFFED ARTICHOKES

Pictured on page 47—

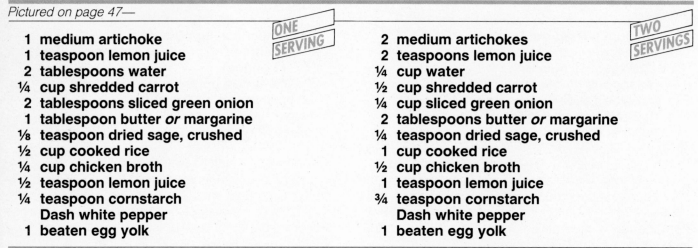

ONE SERVING

- 1 **medium artichoke**
- 1 **teaspoon lemon juice**
- 2 **tablespoons water**
- ¼ **cup shredded carrot**
- 2 **tablespoons sliced green onion**
- 1 **tablespoon butter** *or* **margarine**
- ⅛ **teaspoon dried sage, crushed**
- ½ **cup cooked rice**
- ¼ **cup chicken broth**
- ½ **teaspoon lemon juice**
- ¼ **teaspoon cornstarch**
-   **Dash white pepper**
- 1 **beaten egg yolk**

TWO SERVINGS

- 2 **medium artichokes**
- 2 **teaspoons lemon juice**
- ¼ **cup water**
- ½ **cup shredded carrot**
- ¼ **cup sliced green onion**
- 2 **tablespoons butter** *or* **margarine**
- ¼ **teaspoon dried sage, crushed**
- 1 **cup cooked rice**
- ½ **cup chicken broth**
- 1 **teaspoon lemon juice**
- ¾ **teaspoon cornstarch**
-   **Dash white pepper**
- 1 **beaten egg yolk**

Cut off stem and loose outer leaves from artichoke. Cut off 1 inch from top. Snip off sharp leaf tips. Brush cut edges with 1 teaspoon lemon juice. Place artichoke and water in a small casserole. Cover with vented clear plastic wrap. Micro-cook, covered, on 100% power for 5 to 7 minutes or just till tender, rotating casserole a half-turn after 3 minutes. Let stand, covered, while preparing stuffing.

For stuffing, in a small nonmetal bowl stir together carrot, onion, butter or margarine, and sage. Micro-cook, covered, on 100% power for 1½ to 2½ minutes or till vegetables are tender, stirring once. Stir together vegetable mixture and rice.

Drain artichoke. Remove center leaves and choke from artichoke. Spread the artichoke leaves slightly. Spoon rice stuffing into the center of the artichoke and behind each large leaf. Return artichoke to casserole. Cover with vented clear plastic wrap. Micro-cook, covered, on 100% power for 1 to 2 minutes or till stuffing is hot and base of artichoke is fork-tender, rotating the casserole a half-turn every 30 seconds. Let stand, covered, while preparing sauce.

For sauce, in a 1-cup measure stir together chicken broth, ½ teaspoon lemon juice, cornstarch, and pepper. Micro-cook, uncovered, on 100% power for 1 to 2 minutes or till thickened and bubbly, stirring every 30 seconds. Stir *half* of the hot mixture into the egg yolk. Return all to the 1-cup measure. Micro-cook, uncovered, on 100% power for 15 seconds. Transfer stuffed artichoke to a warm plate. Pour sauce around the artichoke. Makes 1 serving.

Cut off stems and loose outer leaves from artichokes. Cut off 1 inch from tops. Snip off sharp leaf tips. Brush cut edges with 2 teaspoons lemon juice. Place artichokes and water in a casserole. Cover with vented clear plastic wrap. Micro-cook, covered, on 100% power for 7 to 9 minutes or just till tender, rotating casserole a half-turn after 4 minutes. Let stand, covered, while preparing stuffing.

For stuffing, in a small nonmetal bowl stir together carrot, onion, butter or margarine, and sage. Micro-cook, covered, on 100% power for 2½ to 3½ minutes or till vegetables are tender, stirring once. Stir together vegetable mixture and rice.

Drain artichokes. Remove the center leaves and chokes from artichokes. Spread artichoke leaves slightly. Spoon rice stuffing into the center of each artichoke and behind each large leaf. Return artichokes to casserole. Cover with vented clear plastic wrap. Micro-cook, covered, on 100% power for 2 to 3 minutes or till stuffing is hot and bases of artichokes are fork-tender, rotating the casserole a half-turn every minute. Let stand, covered, while preparing sauce.

For sauce, in a 2-cup measure stir together chicken broth, 1 teaspoon lemon juice, cornstarch, and pepper. Micro-cook, uncovered, on 100% power for 2 to 3 minutes or till thickened and bubbly, stirring every 30 seconds. Stir *half* of the hot mixture into the egg yolk. Return all to the 2-cup measure. Micro-cook, uncovered, on 100% power for 30 seconds. Transfer stuffed artichokes to a warm serving platter. Pour sauce around the artichokes. Makes 2 servings.

Preparing an Artichoke: To prepare an artichoke for micro-cooking, cut off the stem, remove the loose outer leaves, and cut off one inch from the top of the artichoke. Use kitchen shears to snip off the sharp artichoke leaf tips, as shown in the photo. Then brush the cut edges with lemon juice to prevent browning.

Removing the Choke: After micro-cooking the arti-choke, it's easiest to remove the choke by using a spoon to reach down into the center of the artichoke and scoop out the fuzzy choke portion.

Stuffing the Artichoke: Stuff the artichoke by using a spoon to place the rice stuffing in the center and be-hind each large leaf of the artichoke.

SWISS-SAUCED BROCCOLI

ONE SERVING

- 3 ounces fresh broccoli
- 1 tablespoon water
  Dash salt
- 1 teaspoon butter *or* margarine
- 1 teaspoon all-purpose flour
  Dash salt
  Dash white pepper
- ¼ cup milk
- 2 tablespoons shredded Swiss cheese

TWO SERVINGS

- 6 ounces fresh broccoli
- 2 tablespoons water
- ⅛ teaspoon salt
- 2 teaspoons butter *or* margarine
- 1½ teaspoons all-purpose flour
  Dash salt
  Dash white pepper
- ⅓ cup milk
- ¼ cup shredded Swiss cheese (1 ounce)

Wash broccoli; remove outer leaves and tough part of stalks. Cut the broccoli stalks lengthwise into uniform spears, following the branching lines. In a 20-ounce casserole combine the broccoli spears, water, and dash salt. Micro-cook, covered, on 100% power for 3 to 4 minutes or just till tender. Let stand, covered, while preparing sauce.

For sauce, in a 1-cup measure micro-cook butter or margarine, uncovered, on 100% power for 20 to 30 seconds or till melted. Stir in flour, dash salt, and pepper. Stir in milk. Micro-cook, uncovered, on 100% power for 45 seconds to 1½ minutes or till thickened and bubbly, stirring every 30 seconds. Stir in shredded Swiss cheese till melted. Drain broccoli. Serve sauce atop broccoli. Makes 1 serving.

Wash broccoli; remove outer leaves and tough part of stalks. Cut broccoli stalks lengthwise into uniform spears, following the branching lines. In a 1-quart casserole combine broccoli, water, and ⅛ teaspoon salt. Micro-cook, covered, on 100% power for 5 to 6 minutes or just till tender. Let stand, covered, while preparing sauce.

For sauce, in a 1-cup measure micro-cook butter or margarine, uncovered, on 100% power for 30 to 40 seconds or till melted. Stir in flour, dash salt, and pepper. Stir in milk. Micro-cook, uncovered, on 100% power for 1 to 2 minutes or till thickened and bubbly, stirring every 30 seconds. Stir in shredded Swiss cheese till melted. Drain broccoli. Serve sauce atop broccoli. Makes 2 servings.

GREEN BEANS AMANDINE

ONE SERVING

- ½ cup frozen cut green beans
- 1 teaspoon water
- 1 teaspoon butter *or* margarine
- 1 tablespoon slivered almonds, toasted
- ¼ teaspoon lemon juice

TWO SERVINGS

- 1 cup frozen cut green beans
- 2 teaspoons water
- 2 teaspoons butter *or* margarine
- 2 tablespoons slivered almonds, toasted
- ½ teaspoon lemon juice

Place green beans in a small nonmetal bowl. Sprinkle with water. Micro-cook, covered, on 100% power for 3 to 4 minutes or just till tender. Let stand, covered, while preparing butter mixture.

For butter mixture, in a custard cup micro-cook butter or margarine, uncovered, on 100% power for 20 to 30 seconds or till melted. Stir in toasted almonds and lemon juice. Drain green beans; spoon butter mixture over green beans. Makes 1 serving.

Place green beans in a small nonmetal bowl. Sprinkle with water. Micro-cook, covered, on 100% power for 5 to 6 minutes or just till tender. Let stand, covered, while preparing butter mixture.

For butter mixture, in a custard cup micro-cook butter or margarine, uncovered, on 100% power for 30 to 45 seconds or till melted. Stir in toasted almonds and lemon juice. Drain green beans; spoon butter mixture over green beans. Makes 2 servings.

•
Rice-Stuffed Artichokes is an elegant vegetable dish to serve with beef, pork, or poultry (see recipe, page 44).

CITRUS DUMPLINGS

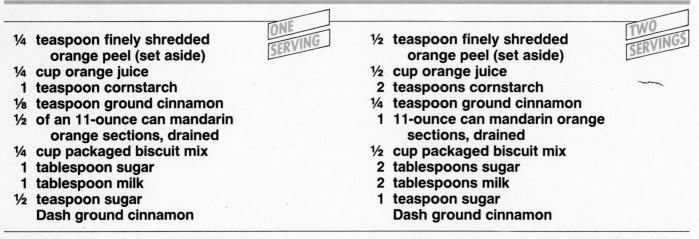

ONE SERVING

¼ teaspoon finely shredded
orange peel (set aside)
¼ cup orange juice
1 teaspoon cornstarch
⅛ teaspoon ground cinnamon
½ of an 11-ounce can mandarin
orange sections, drained
¼ cup packaged biscuit mix
1 tablespoon sugar
1 tablespoon milk
½ teaspoon sugar
Dash ground cinnamon

TWO SERVINGS

½ teaspoon finely shredded
orange peel (set aside)
½ cup orange juice
2 teaspoons cornstarch
¼ teaspoon ground cinnamon
1 11-ounce can mandarin orange
sections, drained
½ cup packaged biscuit mix
2 tablespoons sugar
2 tablespoons milk
1 teaspoon sugar
Dash ground cinnamon

In a 20-ounce casserole stir together orange juice, cornstarch, and ⅛ teaspoon ground cinnamon. Micro-cook, uncovered, on 100% power for 1 to 1½ minutes or till thickened and bubbly, stirring every 30 seconds. Stir in the drained mandarin orange sections and finely shredded orange peel. Micro-cook, uncovered, on 100% power for 30 seconds to 1 minute or till mixture is heated through.

Meanwhile, for dumplings, stir together packaged biscuit mix and 1 tablespoon sugar. Add milk, stirring just till moistened. Drop mixture into two mounds atop the hot orange mixture. Micro-cook, uncovered, on 50% power for 4 to 5 minutes or till dumplings are just set. Stir together the ½ teaspoon sugar and dash ground cinnamon. Sprinkle sugar mixture atop dumplings. Makes 1 serving.

In a 1-quart casserole stir together orange juice, cornstarch, and ¼ teaspoon ground cinnamon. Micro-cook, uncovered, on 100% power for 1½ to 2 minutes or till thickened and bubbly, stirring every 30 seconds. Stir in drained mandarin orange sections and finely shredded orange peel. Micro-cook, uncovered, on 100% power for 1 to 1½ minutes or till mixture is heated through.

Meanwhile, for dumplings, stir together packaged biscuit mix and 2 tablespoons sugar. Add milk, stirring just till moistened. Drop mixture into four mounds atop the hot orange mixture. Micro-cook, uncovered, on 50% power for 6 to 7 minutes or till dumplings are just set. Stir together the 1 teaspoon sugar and dash ground cinnamon. Sprinkle sugar mixture atop dumplings. Makes 2 servings.

STIRRED CUSTARD SAUCE

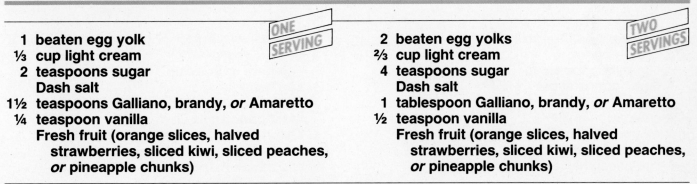

ONE SERVING	**TWO SERVINGS**
1 **beaten egg yolk**	2 **beaten egg yolks**
⅓ **cup light cream**	⅔ **cup light cream**
2 **teaspoons sugar**	4 **teaspoons sugar**
Dash salt	**Dash salt**
1½ **teaspoons Galliano, brandy, *or* Amaretto**	1 **tablespoon Galliano, brandy, *or* Amaretto**
¼ **teaspoon vanilla**	½ **teaspoon vanilla**
Fresh fruit (orange slices, halved strawberries, sliced kiwi, sliced peaches, *or* pineapple chunks)	**Fresh fruit (orange slices, halved strawberries, sliced kiwi, sliced peaches, *or* pineapple chunks)**

In a 1-cup measure stir together egg yolk, light cream, sugar, and salt. Micro-cook, uncovered, on 50% power for 1½ to 2 minutes or till mixture thickens slightly, stirring every 30 seconds. Place the 1-cup measure in a bowl of ice water and stir egg yolk mixture for 2 minutes. Stir in Galliano, brandy, or Amaretto and vanilla. Cover surface of mixture with clear plastic wrap and refrigerate till serving time. To serve, spoon over fresh fruit. Makes 1 serving.

In a 2-cup measure stir together egg yolks, light cream, sugar, and salt. Micro-cook, uncovered, on 50% power for 3 to 5 minutes or till mixture thickens slightly, stirring every minute. Place the 2-cup measure in a bowl of ice water and stir egg yolk mixture for 2 minutes. Stir in Galliano, brandy, or Amaretto and vanilla. Cover surface of mixture with clear plastic wrap and refrigerate till serving time. To serve, spoon over fresh fruit. Makes 2 servings.

Cooling the Custard Sauce: Cool the custard mixture for Stirred Custard Sauce by placing the glass measure inside a larger bowl filled with ice water. After stirring the mixture, stir in the Galliano, brandy, or Amaretto and the vanilla. Adding these ingredients at this stage speeds the cooling of the custard and helps prevent curdling. Be sure to place clear plastic wrap directly on the surface of the custard before it is refrigerated. Covering the surface will prevent a "skin" from forming on the top of the custard sauce.

PECAN PIE

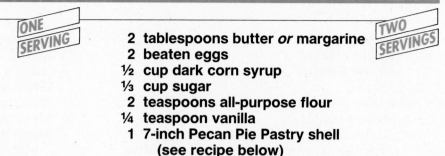

ONE SERVING	TWO SERVINGS

1 tablespoon butter *or* margarine
1 beaten egg
¼ cup dark corn syrup
3 tablespoons sugar
1 teaspoon all-purpose flour
⅛ teaspoon vanilla
1 4½-inch Pecan Pie Pastry shell
   (see recipe below)
¼ cup pecan halves
	2 tablespoons butter *or* margarine
	2 beaten eggs
	½ cup dark corn syrup
	⅓ cup sugar
	2 teaspoons all-purpose flour
	¼ teaspoon vanilla
	1 7-inch Pecan Pie Pastry shell
	   (see recipe below)
	½ cup pecan halves

In a small nonmetal bowl micro-cook butter or margarine, uncovered, on 100% power for 20 to 30 seconds or till melted. Stir in the beaten egg, corn syrup, sugar, and flour. Micro-cook, uncovered, on 50% power for 3 to 3½ minutes or till slightly thickened, stirring every 30 seconds. Stir in vanilla. Turn into Pecan Pie Pastry. Arrange pecan halves atop. Micro-cook, uncovered, on 30% power for 1½ to 2 minutes or just till set, rotating the dish a quarter-turn every minute. Cool before serving. Makes 1 serving.

In a small nonmetal bowl micro-cook butter or margarine, uncovered, on 100% power for 30 seconds to 1 minute or till melted. Stir in beaten eggs, corn syrup, sugar, and flour. Micro-cook, uncovered, on 50% power about 5 minutes or till slightly thickened, stirring every minute. Stir in vanilla. Turn into Pecan Pie Pastry. Arrange pecan halves atop. Micro-cook, uncovered, on 30% power for 6 to 7 minutes* or just till set, rotating the dish a quarter-turn every 2 minutes. Cool before serving. Makes 2 servings.

*Note: The final micro-cooking time for the 2-serving version is considerably longer than the final micro-cooking time for the 1-serving version.

PECAN PIE PASTRY

ONE SERVING	TWO SERVINGS

¼ cup all-purpose flour
1 tablespoon finely
   chopped pecans
⅛ teaspoon salt
5 teaspoons shortening *or* lard
2 to 2½ teaspoons cold water
   Dried beans
	½ cup all-purpose flour
	2 tablespoons finely
	   chopped pecans
	¼ teaspoon salt
	3 tablespoons shortening *or* lard
	4 to 5 teaspoons cold water
	   Dried beans

In a small mixing bowl stir together flour, chopped pecans, and salt. Cut in shortening or lard till the pieces are the size of small peas. Sprinkle some of the cold water over part of the mixture; gently toss with a fork. Push to side of bowl. Repeat till all is moistened. Form dough into a ball. On a lightly floured surface roll the ball into a 7-inch circle. Line a 4½-inch quiche dish or pie plate with the pastry. Flute edge. Cover surface of pastry with clear plastic wrap. Spread dried beans atop the plastic wrap to a depth of 1 inch.

Micro-cook, uncovered, on 70% power for 5 minutes, rotating the dish a half-turn every minute. Carefully lift plastic wrap and beans from pastry. Micro-cook pastry, uncovered, on 70% power about 1 minute or till pastry is dry. Makes one 4½-inch pastry shell.

In a small mixing bowl stir together flour, chopped pecans, and salt. Cut in shortening or lard till the pieces are the size of small peas. Sprinkle some of the cold water over part of the mixture; gently toss with a fork. Push to side of bowl. Repeat till all is moistened. Form dough into a ball. On a lightly floured surface roll the ball into a 10-inch circle. Line a 7-inch pie plate or quiche dish with the pastry. Flute edge. Cover surface of pastry with clear plastic wrap. Spread dried beans atop the plastic wrap to a depth of 1 inch.

Micro-cook, uncovered, on 70% power for 6 minutes, rotating the dish a half-turn every 2 minutes. Carefully lift plastic wrap and beans from pastry. Micro-cook, uncovered, on 70% power about 2 minutes or till pastry is dry. Makes one 7-inch pastry shell.

CHOCOLATE POTS DE CRÈME

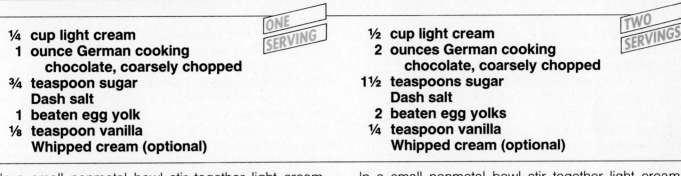

ONE SERVING	TWO SERVINGS
¼ cup light cream	½ cup light cream
1 ounce German cooking chocolate, coarsely chopped	2 ounces German cooking chocolate, coarsely chopped
¾ teaspoon sugar	1½ teaspoons sugar
Dash salt	Dash salt
1 beaten egg yolk	2 beaten egg yolks
⅛ teaspoon vanilla	¼ teaspoon vanilla
Whipped cream (optional)	Whipped cream (optional)

In a small nonmetal bowl stir together light cream, chopped chocolate, sugar, and salt. Micro-cook, uncovered, on 100% power about 1 minute or till the chocolate is melted, stirring after 30 seconds. Stir about *half* of the hot mixture into the beaten egg yolk. Return all to the bowl, mixing well. Micro-cook, uncovered, on 50% power for 1 to 2 minutes or till thickened, stirring every 15 seconds. Stir in vanilla. Pour into pot de crème cup or 6-ounce custard cup. Cover and chill for several hours or till firm. Garnish with whipped cream, if desired. Makes 1 serving.

In a small nonmetal bowl stir together light cream, chopped chocolate, sugar, and salt. Micro-cook, uncovered, on 100% power about 1½ minutes or till the chocolate is melted, stirring every 30 seconds. Stir about *half* of the hot mixture into the beaten egg yolks. Return all to the bowl, mixing well. Micro-cook, uncovered, on 50% power for 2 to 3 minutes or till thickened, stirring every 30 seconds. Stir in vanilla. Pour into two pot de crème cups or 6-ounce custard cups. Cover and chill for several hours or till firm. Garnish with whipped cream, if desired. Makes 2 servings.

Selecting the Right Chocolate: You'll find three basic types of chocolate in the baking supplies department of most supermarkets—semisweet chocolate, unsweetened chocolate, and sweet chocolate. The semisweet chocolate is made from chocolate that is just slightly sweetened with sugar. Unsweetened chocolate is the original baking or cooking chocolate and has no added flavorings or sugar. And sweet chocolate, such as the German cooking chocolate used in the Chocolate Pots de Crème recipe, is chocolate mixed with sugar and sometimes additional cocoa butter or flavorings.

BANANA SPLIT SUNDAES

ONE SERVING

1 square (1 ounce)
   semisweet chocolate
2 tablespoons light corn syrup
2 tablespoons Eagle Brand
   sweetened condensed milk
⅛ teaspoon vanilla
   Ice cream
1 tablespoon peanuts
1 small ripe banana, quartered

TWO SERVINGS

2 squares (2 ounces)
   semisweet chocolate
¼ cup light corn syrup
¼ cup Eagle Brand sweetened
   condensed milk
¼ teaspoon vanilla
   Ice cream
2 tablespoons peanuts
2 small ripe bananas, quartered

Place chocolate in a 2-cup measure. Micro-cook, uncovered, on 100% power for 1½ to 2 minutes or till melted, stirring once. Stir in corn syrup and sweetened condensed milk. Micro-cook, uncovered, on 100% power for 30 to 45 seconds or till heated through. Stir in vanilla. Serve warm atop ice cream. Sprinkle with peanuts. Arrange the quartered banana around ice cream. Makes 1 serving.

Place chocolate in a 2-cup measure. Micro-cook, uncovered, on 100% power for 2 to 3 minutes or till melted, stirring once. Stir in corn syrup and sweetened condensed milk. Micro-cook, uncovered, on 100% power for 45 seconds to 1 minute or till heated through. Stir in vanilla. Serve warm atop ice cream. Sprinkle with peanuts. Arrange quartered bananas around ice cream. Makes 2 servings.

Selecting Ripe Bananas: When buying bananas for Banana Split Sundaes, look for good quality bananas that are bright, plump, firm, and free of bruises or large blemishes. The color may range from green to yellow with brown flecks. Green bananas are underripe. Those that are lightly brown-flecked are at the optimum stage of ripeness. If you won't be using them for a day or two, select bananas that are not quite ripe. They will continue ripening at home when stored at room temperature. Always avoid any with grayish skin color, an indication of chill damage.

Celebrate a good report card or other special occasion by savoring Banana Split Sundaes.

PECAN PUDDING

ONE SERVING	TWO SERVINGS
2 teaspoons butter *or* margarine	1 tablespoon butter *or* margarine
1 beaten egg	1 beaten egg
3 tablespoons dark corn syrup	⅓ cup dark corn syrup
⅛ teaspoon vanilla	¼ teaspoon vanilla
1 tablespoon all-purpose flour	2 tablespoons all-purpose flour
Dash baking powder	⅛ teaspoon baking powder
2 tablespoons chopped pecans	¼ cup chopped pecans
Powdered sugar	Powdered sugar

ONE SERVING

In a 10-ounce custard cup micro-cook the butter or margarine, uncovered, on 100% power for 15 to 30 seconds or just till melted. Swirl the butter in the custard cup, coating the sides and bottom. Pour the excess butter from the custard cup into the beaten egg. Stir in the dark corn syrup and vanilla.

Stir together flour and baking powder. Stir flour mixture into egg mixture. Gently fold in chopped pecans. Pour the pecan mixture into the buttered 10-ounce custard cup. Micro-cook, uncovered, on 50% power for 2 to 2½ minutes or till the pecan mixture is just set, rotating the custard cup a half-turn every minute. Sift a little powdered sugar atop. Serve warm with light cream, if desired. Makes 1 serving.

TWO SERVINGS

In a 15-ounce custard cup micro-cook the butter or margarine, uncovered, on 100% power for 30 to 40 seconds or just till melted. Swirl the butter in the custard cup, coating the sides and bottom. Pour the excess butter from the custard cup into the beaten egg. Stir in the dark corn syrup and vanilla.

Stir together flour and baking powder. Stir flour mixture into egg mixture. Gently fold in chopped pecans. Pour the pecan mixture into the buttered 15-ounce custard cup. Micro-cook, uncovered, on 50% power for 3 to 4 minutes or till the pecan mixture is just set, rotating the custard cup a half-turn every minute. Sift a little powdered sugar atop. Serve warm with light cream, if desired. Makes 2 servings.

CHILI CON QUESO

ONE SERVING	TWO SERVINGS
2 tablespoons chopped onion	¼ cup chopped onion
½ teaspoon butter *or* margarine	1 teaspoon butter *or* margarine
¼ cup American cheese spread	½ cup American cheese spread
1 small tomato, peeled, seeded, and chopped	1 medium tomato, peeled, seeded, and chopped
1 tablespoon chopped canned green chili peppers	2 tablespoons chopped canned green chili peppers
Dash bottled hot pepper sauce (optional)	Dash bottled hot pepper sauce (optional)
Tortilla chips *or* corn chips	Tortilla chips *or* corn chips

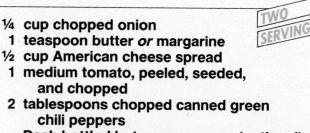

ONE SERVING

In a small nonmetal bowl micro-cook the chopped onion and butter or margarine, uncovered, on 100% power for 1 to 1½ minutes or till the onion is tender but not brown.

Stir in the American cheese spread. Micro-cook, uncovered, on 100% power about 1 minute or till the cheese spread is melted, stirring occasionally. Stir in chopped tomato, green chili peppers, and bottled hot pepper sauce, if desired.

Micro-cook the cheese mixture, uncovered, on 100% power for 20 to 40 seconds more or till the cheese mixture is heated through. Serve immediately with tortilla chips or corn chips. Makes about ½ cup cheese mixture.

TWO SERVINGS

In a small nonmetal bowl micro-cook the chopped onion and butter or margarine, uncovered, on 100% power for 1½ to 2 minutes or till the onion is tender but not brown.

Stir in the American cheese spread. Micro-cook, uncovered, on 100% power for 2 to 3 minutes or till the cheese spread is melted, stirring occasionally. Stir in chopped tomato, green chili peppers, and bottled hot pepper sauce, if desired.

Micro-cook the cheese mixture, uncovered, on 100% power for 30 seconds to 1 minute more or till the cheese mixture is heated through. Serve immediately with tortilla chips or corn chips. Makes about 1 cup cheese mixture.

Removing the Cheese Rind: To remove the rind from the Brie or Camembert cheese, use a sharp paring knife and cut away a thin portion from the outside edge. Also, cut away a thin portion from both the top and bottom of the cheese round.

Micro-Cooking the Nutty Cheese Brûlée: When the cheese brûlée is ready, it should be soft enough for dipping and starting to lose its shape. You can serve it as a snack or dessert with sliced fruits and flat bread or crackers.

NUTTY CHEESE BRÛLÉE

ONE SERVING

½ of a 4-ounce package Brie cheese, rind removed, *or* ½ of a 5¼-ounce can Camembert cheese, rind removed
2 teaspoons strawberry, pineapple, *or* chocolate ice cream topping
1 tablespoon broken pecans *or* broken walnuts
Flat bread *or* unsalted crackers
Apple slices *or* pear slices

Place the Brie or Camembert cheese in the center of a nonmetal plate or small shallow baking dish. Spoon the ice cream topping over the cheese. Sprinkle with pecans or walnuts. Micro-cook, uncovered, on 100% power about 15 seconds or till the cheese begins to melt and lose its shape. Serve immediately with flat bread or unsalted crackers and apple or pear slices. Makes 1 serving.

TWO SERVINGS

1 4-ounce package Brie cheese, rind removed, *or* one 5¼-ounce can Camembert cheese, rind removed
1 tablespoon strawberry, pineapple, *or* chocolate ice cream topping
2 tablespoons broken pecans *or* broken walnuts
Flat bread *or* unsalted crackers
Apple slices *or* pear slices

Place the Brie or Camembert cheese in the center of a nonmetal plate or small shallow baking dish. Spoon the ice cream topping over the cheese. Sprinkle with pecans or walnuts. Micro-cook, uncovered, on 100% power about 30 seconds or till the cheese begins to melt and lose its shape. Serve immediately with flat bread or unsalted crackers and apple or pear slices. Makes 2 servings.

IRISH COFFEE

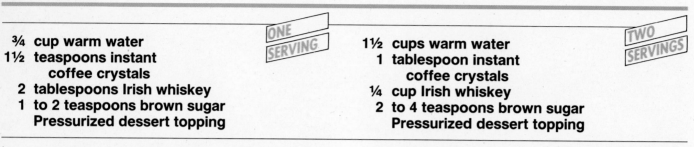

¾	cup warm water
1½	teaspoons instant
	coffee crystals
2	tablespoons Irish whiskey
1	to 2 teaspoons brown sugar
	Pressurized dessert topping

In a nonmetal mug combine water and instant coffee crystals. Micro-cook, uncovered, on 100% power about 1½ minutes or just till steaming hot. Stir in Irish whiskey and brown sugar. Top with pressurized dessert topping. Makes 1 (8-ounce) serving.

1½	cups warm water
1	tablespoon instant
	coffee crystals
¼	cup Irish whiskey
2	to 4 teaspoons brown sugar
	Pressurized dessert topping

In a 2-cup measure combine water and instant coffee crystals. Micro-cook, uncovered, on 100% power about 4 minutes or just till steaming hot. Stir in Irish whiskey and brown sugar. Serve in mugs. Top each mug of coffee mixture with some pressurized dessert topping. Makes 2 (8-ounce) servings.

AMARETTO COFFEE

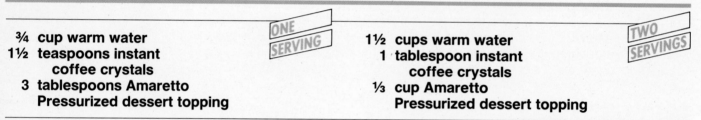

¾	cup warm water
1½	teaspoons instant
	coffee crystals
3	tablespoons Amaretto
	Pressurized dessert topping

In a nonmetal mug stir together water and instant coffee crystals. Micro-cook, uncovered, on 100% power about 1½ minutes or just till mixture is steaming hot. Stir in Amaretto. Top with pressurized dessert topping. Makes 1 (8-ounce) serving.

1½	cups warm water
1	tablespoon instant
	coffee crystals
⅓	cup Amaretto
	Pressurized dessert topping

In a 2-cup measure stir together water and instant coffee crystals. Micro-cook, uncovered, on 100% power about 4 minutes or just till mixture is steaming hot. Stir in Amaretto. Serve in mugs. Top each mug of coffee mixture with some dessert topping. Makes 2 (8-ounce) servings.

LEMON SPICE TEA

1	cup warm water
1½	teaspoons honey
1	slice lemon
1	inch stick cinnamon, broken up
1	tea bag
	Lemon slice (optional)

In a nonmetal mug combine water, honey, lemon slice, and cinnamon. Micro-cook mixture, uncovered, on 100% power about 1½ minutes or just till steaming hot. Add tea bag. Cover and steep for 4 minutes. Remove tea bag, lemon slice, and cinnamon. Garnish with an additional lemon slice, if desired. Makes 1 (8-ounce) serving.

2	cups warm water
1	tablespoon honey
2	slices lemon
2	inches stick cinnamon, broken up
2	tea bags
	Lemon slices (optional)

In a 2-cup measure combine water, honey, lemon slices, and cinnamon. Micro-cook, uncovered, on 100% power about 4 minutes or just till steaming hot. Add the tea bags. Cover and steep for 4 minutes. Remove tea bags, lemon slices, and cinnamon. Pour into 2 mugs. Garnish with additional lemon slices, if desired. Makes 2 (8-ounce) servings.

HOT CHOCOLATE RUM

1 cup warm water
1 envelope instant cocoa mix
2 tablespoons rum
Pressurized dessert topping (optional)
Chocolate sprinkles (optional)

2 cups warm water
2 envelopes instant cocoa mix
¼ cup rum
Pressurized dessert topping (optional)
Chocolate sprinkles (optional)

In a 2-cup measure micro-cook water, uncovered, on 100% power for 1½ to 2 minutes or till steaming hot. Stir in cocoa mix and rum. Serve in a mug. Garnish with pressurized dessert topping and chocolate sprinkles, if desired. Makes 1 (10-ounce) serving.

In a 4-cup measure micro-cook water, uncovered, on 100% power for 4 to 5 minutes or till steaming hot. Stir in cocoa mix and rum. Serve in mugs. Garnish with pressurized dessert topping and chocolate sprinkles, if desired. Makes 2 (10-ounce) servings.

CIDER SNAP

1 cup apple cider *or* apple juice
2 teaspoons red
   cinnamon candies
2 thin apple slices (optional)

2 cups apple cider *or* apple juice
4 teaspoons red
   cinnamon candies
4 thin apple slices (optional)

In a nonmetal mug combine apple cider and cinnamon candies. Micro-cook, uncovered, on 100% power for 1½ to 2 minutes or till candies dissolve and the cider is steaming hot, stirring once. Garnish with apple slices, if desired. Makes 1 (8-ounce) serving.

In a 4-cup measure combine apple cider and cinnamon candies. Micro-cook, uncovered, on 100% power for 4 to 5 minutes or till candies dissolve and the cider is steaming hot, stirring once. Serve in mugs. Garnish with apple slices, if desired. Makes 2 (8-ounce) servings.

GLOGG

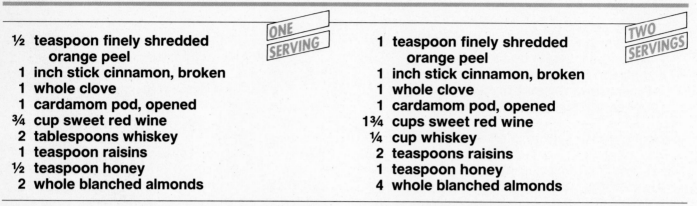

ONE SERVING

- ½ teaspoon finely shredded orange peel
- 1 inch stick cinnamon, broken
- 1 whole clove
- 1 cardamom pod, opened
- ¾ cup sweet red wine
- 2 tablespoons whiskey
- 1 teaspoon raisins
- ½ teaspoon honey
- 2 whole blanched almonds

TWO SERVINGS

- 1 teaspoon finely shredded orange peel
- 1 inch stick cinnamon, broken
- 1 whole clove
- 1 cardamom pod, opened
- 1¾ cups sweet red wine
- ¼ cup whiskey
- 2 teaspoons raisins
- 1 teaspoon honey
- 4 whole blanched almonds

For spice bag, tie shredded orange peel, cinnamon, whole clove, and opened cardamom pod in cheesecloth. In a 2-cup measure combine wine, whiskey, raisins, honey, and spice bag. Micro-cook, uncovered, on 50% power for 3 to 4 minutes or till heated through, but not boiling. If desired, cover and let stand at room temperature for 2 to 3 hours to develop more flavor. If wine mixture is allowed to stand, micro-cook, uncovered, on 50% power for 3 to 4 minutes more or till heated through, but not boiling. Remove spice bag. Serve in a mug. Add almonds. Makes about 1 (6-ounce) serving.

For spice bag, tie orange peel, stick cinnamon, whole clove, and opened cardamom pod in cheesecloth. In a 4-cup measure combine wine, whiskey, raisins, honey, and spice bag. Micro-cook, uncovered, on 50% power about 6 minutes or till heated through, but not boiling. If desired, cover and let stand at room temperature for 2 to 3 hours to develop more flavor. If wine mixture is allowed to stand, micro-cook, uncovered, on 50% power about 6 minutes more or till heated through, but not boiling. Remove spice bag. Serve in mugs. Add some almonds to each mug. Makes about 2 (7-ounce) servings.

Tieing Spice Bags: To tie the spices for hot Glogg in a cheesecloth bag, place the shredded orange peel, stick cinnamon, whole clove, and opened cardamom pod on a double thickness of cheesecloth. Bring the cheesecloth up around the spices and tie it closed with a piece of string. The spice bag is then added to the other ingredients and micro-cooked. If you want to allow the wine mixture to develop more flavor, allow it to stand at room temperature with the spice bag in it for 2 to 3 hours. Micro-cook the wine mixture again, with the spice bag still in it, then remove and discard the bag before serving the hot Glogg.

HOT CHOCOLATE FLOAT

1 cup warm water
1 envelope instant cocoa mix
  Chocolate-chip mint ice cream
  or peppermint ice cream

2 cups warm water
2 envelopes instant cocoa mix
  Chocolate-chip mint ice cream
  or peppermint ice cream

In a 2-cup measure micro-cook water, uncovered, on 100% power for 1½ to 2 minutes or till steaming hot. Stir in cocoa mix. Pour into a mug. Top hot chocolate with a small scoop of ice cream. Serve immediately. Makes 1 (10- to 12-ounce) serving.

In a 4-cup measure micro-cook water, uncovered, on 100% power for 4 to 5 minutes or till steaming hot. Stir in the cocoa mix. Pour into two mugs. Top the hot chocolate mixture in each mug with a small scoop of ice cream. Serve immediately. Makes 2 (10- to 12-ounce) servings.

HOT BUTTERED RUM

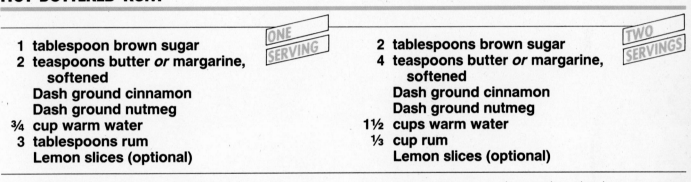

1 tablespoon brown sugar
2 teaspoons butter *or* margarine,
  softened
  Dash ground cinnamon
  Dash ground nutmeg
¾ cup warm water
3 tablespoons rum
  Lemon slices (optional)

2 tablespoons brown sugar
4 teaspoons butter *or* margarine,
  softened
  Dash ground cinnamon
  Dash ground nutmeg
1½ cups warm water
⅓ cup rum
  Lemon slices (optional)

In a nonmetal mug stir together the brown sugar, butter or margarine, cinnamon, and nutmeg. Stir in the warm water. Micro-cook, uncovered, on 100% power for 1 to 1½ minutes or till steaming hot. Stir in the rum. Garnish with lemon slices, if desired. Makes 1 (8-ounce) serving.

In a 2-cup measure stir together the brown sugar, butter or margarine, cinnamon, and nutmeg. Stir in the warm water. Micro-cook, uncovered, on 100% power for 3 to 4 minutes or till steaming hot. Stir in the rum. Serve in mugs. Garnish with lemon slices, if desired. Makes 2 (8-ounce) servings.

PLANNED-OVER RECIPES

What do you do when you usually cook for one or two and the smallest package of meat or poultry you can buy is enough to serve three or four? Do you eat hamburgers two nights in a row or fried chicken for an entire week?

It can be a problem, but we've solved it. We've taken the smallest package size you can buy of several foods and divided each into the right amounts for one- or two-serving recipes. For example, in this chapter you'll find four recipes that use ground beef—*Meatball Sandwiches, Hamburger Casserole, Salisbury Steak, and Cheeseburger Meat Loaves* (see the Index for recipe pages). By using these recipes, you can use up your ground beef without having to eat the same thing every night. In addition we've included recipes that use the smallest common unit or package size of other meats, fruits, fresh vegetables, frozen vegetables, cake mix, and more.

HAMBURGER CASSEROLE

Pictured on page 61—

- ½ pound lean ground beef
- ¼ cup thinly sliced celery
- 2 tablespoons chopped onion
- 1 7½-ounce can semicondensed cream of mushroom soup
- ¼ cup dairy sour cream
- 4 teaspoons snipped parsley
- ¼ teaspoon dried basil, crushed
- 1 cup cooked medium noodles
- 1½ teaspoons butter *or* margarine
- ¼ cup finely crushed rich round crackers

Crumble meat into a 1-quart casserole. Add celery and onion. Micro-cook, covered, on 100% power for 3 to 4 minutes or till done, stirring once. Drain off fat. Stir soup, sour cream, *3 teaspoons* of the parsley, and basil into meat mixture. Fold in cooked noodles. Micro-cook, uncovered, on 100% power for 3 to 4 minutes or till heated through, stirring once.

Micro-cook butter or margarine, uncovered, on 100% power about 30 seconds or till melted. Toss with the crushed crackers and remaining parsley. Sprinkle atop the meat mixture. Makes 2 servings.

SALISBURY STEAKS

Pictured on page 61—

- 1 beaten egg
- 3 tablespoons fine dry bread crumbs
- 1½ teaspoons Worcestershire sauce
- ½ pound lean ground beef
- ½ of a 1-ounce envelope brown gravy mix
- ½ of a small onion, sliced and separated into rings
- 2 tablespoons thinly sliced celery

Combine egg, crumbs, Worcestershire sauce, and dash *pepper*. Add beef; mix well. Shape into two ½-inch-thick patties. Place in a 10x6x2-inch baking dish. Cover with waxed paper. Micro-cook, loosely covered, on 100% power for 2 minutes, rotating baking dish a half-turn once. Turn patties over. Micro-cook, loosely covered, on 100% power for 1 to 2 minutes more or till done. Remove patties, reserving drippings in baking dish. Keep patties warm.

Stir gravy mix, onion, celery, and dash *pepper* into reserved drippings. Stir in ½ cup *water*. Micro-cook, uncovered, on 100% power for 3 to 4 minutes or till thickened and bubbly, stirring every minute. Skim off fat. Serve patties atop steamed vegetables, if desired. Spoon gravy mixture over patties. Makes 2 servings.

CHEESEBURGER MEAT LOAVES

Pictured on page 61—

- 1 beaten egg
- ¼ cup fine dry bread crumbs
- 2 tablespoons finely chopped dill pickle
- ¼ teaspoon salt
  Dash pepper
- ½ pound lean ground beef
- 1 ounce cheddar cheese, cut into two 3x½x½-inch sticks
- 2 tablespoons catsup
- ½ teaspoon dry mustard

In a small bowl combine beaten egg, fine dry bread crumbs, chopped pickle, salt, and pepper. Add ground beef; mix well. Divide meat mixture in half. Shape *each* portion of meat mixture around *one* cheese stick to form an individual meat loaf, being sure to completely seal cheese inside the meat. Place the loaves in a 10x6x2-inch baking dish. Micro-cook, uncovered, on 100% power for 4 to 5 minutes or till done, rotating the dish a quarter-turn every minute.

Transfer the meat loaves to a nonmetal serving platter. Combine the catsup and dry mustard. Spoon the catsup mixture atop the meat loaves. Micro-cook, uncovered, on 100% power about 30 seconds or till heated through. Makes 2 servings.

Dressed-Up Cheeseburger Meat Loaves
Cook 1 cup desired frozen *vegetables* according to package directions; drain and keep warm. Prepare packaged instant mashed *potatoes* (enough for 2 servings) according to package directions; keep warm. Meanwhile, prepare the Cheeseburger Meat Loaves as directed above; micro-cook, uncovered, on 100% power for 4 to 5 minutes or till done, rotating dish a quarter-turn every minute. Transfer the loaves to a nonmetal platter; top with catsup mixture. Arrange the vegetables around the loaves. Pipe or spoon mashed potatoes around the meat and vegetables. Micro-cook, uncovered, on 100% power about 1½ minutes or till heated through. Makes 2 servings.

MEATBALL SANDWICHES

Pictured on pages 60 and 61—

- 1 **beaten egg**
- 2 **tablespoons fine dry bread crumbs**
- ¼ **teaspoon salt**
- ⅛ **teaspoon dried oregano, crushed**
  Dash pepper
- ½ **pound lean ground beef**
- 2 **tablespoons chopped green pepper**
- 1 **tablespoon chopped onion**
- 1 **small clove garlic, minced**
- 1 **tablespoon butter *or* margarine**
- ½ **of an 8-ounce can (½ cup)**
  pizza sauce
- ½ **teaspoon cornstarch**
- 2 **individual French-style rolls**
- ¼ **cup shredded mozzarella cheese (1 ounce)**

In a bowl combine the beaten egg, fine dry bread crumbs, salt, oregano, and pepper. Add the lean ground beef; mix well. Use your hands to shape the ground beef mixture into 8 meatballs. Arrange the meatballs in a circle in a 7-inch pie plate. Micro-cook, uncovered, on 100% power for 3 to 5 minutes or till the meatballs are no longer pink, turning the meatballs and rotating the pie plate a half-turn once. Drain off fat.

In a small nonmetal mixing bowl combine the chopped green pepper, chopped onion, minced garlic, and butter or margarine. Micro-cook, uncovered, on 100% power for 1½ to 2 minutes or till the vegetables are tender, stirring once. Stir together the pizza sauce and cornstarch. Stir into the green pepper mixture in the bowl. Micro-cook, uncovered, on 100% power for 1 to 2 minutes or till the mixture is thickened and bubbly, stirring twice.

To assemble the meatball sandwiches, use a sharp knife to cut a thin slice of bread from the tops of the individual French-style rolls. Use a fork to carefully hollow out the bottoms of the rolls, leaving ¼-inch shells. (Save the excess bread from the rolls for another use. For long-term storage, seal in a plastic bag or an airtight container and freeze.)

Place the rolls in a nonmetal serving container. Place *4* meatballs in *each* hollowed-out roll. Spoon the pizza sauce mixture over the meatballs. Sprinkle the shredded mozzarella cheese over the meatballs and pizza sauce mixture. Micro-cook, uncovered, on 100% power for 1 to 1½ minutes or till the mozzarella cheese is melted. Makes 2 servings.

Hollowing Out the Rolls: After removing the tops from the rolls, use a fork to carefully hollow out the bottoms, leaving ¼-inch shells.

Assembling the Sandwiches: Using a fork and spoon, place 4 meatballs in each hollowed-out roll. Top the meatballs with the pizza sauce mixture and sprinkle with shredded mozzarella cheese.

POT ROAST FOR TWO

¼ of a 3-pound boneless beef chuck
    pot roast, cut 2 inches thick (12 ounces)
½ cup beer *or* water
2 teaspoons Worcestershire sauce
1 small clove garlic, minced
1 teaspoon instant beef bouillon granules
¼ teaspoon dried basil
    or dried marjoram, crushed
    Dash pepper
1 medium potato, peeled and quartered
1 medium carrot, cut into julienne strips
1 medium onion, quartered
2 tablespoons water
1 tablespoon all-purpose flour

With a sharp knife trim any excess fat from the pot roast. In a 1-quart casserole stir together the beer or water, Worcestershire sauce, garlic, instant beef bouillon granules, basil or marjoram, and pepper. Add the pot roast. Micro-cook, covered, on 100% power about 3 minutes or till the liquid is boiling. Micro-cook, covered, on 50% power for 20 minutes more.

Turn the pot roast over; add the quartered potato, the carrot strips, and the quartered onion. Micro-cook the meat and vegetables, covered, on 50% power for 10 to 20 minutes or till the meat is done and the vegetables are tender, spooning the liquid over the meat and vegetables once or twice during cooking. Transfer the meat and the vegetables to a serving platter, reserving the juices in the casserole. Keep the meat and vegetables warm.

To make the gravy, carefully pour the reserved juices into a 1-cup measure. Skim the fat from the reserved juices. If necessary, add additional beer or water to the reserved juices to make ½ cup total liquid; return to the casserole. Stir together the 2 tablespoons water and flour; stir into the reserved juice mixture in the casserole. Micro-cook, uncovered, on 100% power for 1½ to 2 minutes or till the mixture is thickened and bubbly, stirring every minute. Micro-cook, uncovered, on 100% power for 30 seconds more. Spoon gravy over the meat and vegetables. Makes 2 servings.

BEER BEEF STEW

¼ of a 3-pound boneless beef chuck
    pot roast, cut into ½-inch cubes
    (12 ounces)
1 medium onion, cut into eighths
1 small clove garlic, minced
1 teaspoon instant beef bouillon granules
½ teaspoon dried basil, crushed
⅛ teaspoon pepper
¾ cup beer
1 medium carrot, thinly sliced
1 stalk celery, sliced
½ of a small green pepper, chopped
¼ cup beer
1 tablespoon all-purpose flour

In a 1½-quart casserole combine the cubed beef, onion, garlic, instant beef bouillon granules, basil, and pepper. Stir in the ¾ cup beer. Micro-cook, covered, on 100% power for 3 minutes. Stir. Micro-cook, covered, on 50% power for 20 minutes more.

Stir the sliced carrot, sliced celery, and chopped green pepper into the beef mixture in the casserole. Micro-cook, covered, on 50% power about 15 minutes or till the meat is done and the vegetables are tender. Stir together the ¼ cup beer and flour; stir into the beef-vegetable mixture. Micro-cook, uncovered, on 100% power for 2 to 3 minutes or till the mixture is thickened and bubbly, stirring every minute. Micro-cook, uncovered, on 100% power for 30 seconds more. Makes 2 servings.

Thinly Slicing Meat: When recipes call for thin slices of meat, as do Barbecue Beef Sandwiches or Stroganoff-Style Beef, there is a simple technique that will make cutting the meat easier and help assure you of uniformly sized pieces. The trick is to partially freeze the meat (or partially thaw the frozen meat) before thinly bias-slicing it across the grain with a sharp knife. Be sure to plan ahead and allow 45 minutes to 1 hour to partially freeze a 1-inch-thick piece of meat.

BARBECUE BEEF SANDWICHES

¼ cup chopped onion
2 tablespoons chopped green pepper
1 tablespoon water
1 tablespoon vinegar
¾ teaspoon dry mustard
¼ teaspoon chili powder
¼ teaspoon dried basil, crushed
⅛ teaspoon celery seed
¼ of a 3-pound boneless beef chuck
    pot roast, cut into thin, bite-size strips
    (12 ounces)
½ of an 8-ounce can (½ cup) tomato sauce
1 teaspoon brown sugar
2 individual French-style rolls, split

In a 1-quart casserole combine the chopped onion, chopped green pepper, water, vinegar, dry mustard, chili powder, basil, and celery seed; mix well. Add the beef strips; toss to coat. Micro-cook, covered, on 100% power for 3 minutes. Stir. Micro-cook, covered, on 50% power for 20 minutes, stirring twice.

Stir the tomato sauce and brown sugar into the meat mixture in the casserole. Micro-cook, covered, on 50% power for 5 to 10 minutes or till the meat is tender, stirring twice. Place the split French-style rolls on a nonmetal plate. Micro-cook, uncovered, on 50% power for 30 to 45 seconds or till the rolls are heated through. Fill the warm rolls with the hot meat mixture. Makes 2 servings.

STROGANOFF-STYLE BEEF

1 tablespoon cooking oil
¼ of a 3-pound boneless beef chuck
    pot roast, cut into thin, bite-size strips
    (12 ounces)
¾ cup sliced fresh mushrooms
1 small onion, sliced and separated into rings
1 small clove garlic, minced
⅔ cup water
½ cup plain yogurt
4 teaspoons all-purpose flour
1 tablespoon tomato paste
¾ teaspoon instant beef bouillon granules
    Hot cooked noodles *or* rice

Preheat a 10-inch microwave browning dish on 100% power for 3 minutes. Add the cooking oil; swirl to coat the dish. Add the beef strips, sliced mushrooms, sliced onion, and minced garlic. Micro-cook, uncovered, on 100% power for 3 to 4 minutes or till the meat is brown, stirring twice. Add the water. Micro-cook, covered, on 50% power for 15 to 20 minutes or till the meat is tender. Skim off fat, if necessary.

Meanwhile, in a small bowl stir together the yogurt and the flour. Stir in the tomato paste and the instant beef bouillon granules. Stir the yogurt-tomato mixture into the meat mixture. Micro-cook, uncovered, on 100% power for 3 to 4 minutes or till the mixture is thickened and bubbly, stirring every minute. Serve over hot cooked noodles or rice. Makes 2 servings.

Micro-Cooking Coated Poultry: Poultry prepared in the microwave oven does not brown well or get crisp in the short amount of time it requires to cook. A simple way to add color, texture, and appeal is to choose from a variety of coatings or toppings for your poultry. The recipe for Berry-Sauced Chicken Legs demonstrates a good way to incorporate a touch of color by spooning a fruit sauce over the chicken pieces. Or try coating the chicken pieces with herbs or one of many crumb mixtures, such as in the Parmesan Chicken Wings recipe.

When micro-cooking any type of poultry, be sure to arrange the thickest, meatiest portions of the pieces to the outside of the dish to allow for more even cooking. When you use a crumb coating mixture, arrange the coated chicken pieces with the most attractive side up and rotate the dish during micro-cooking, but do not turn the chicken pieces over. This helps to keep the crumb coating mixture crisp.

PARMESAN CHICKEN WINGS

2 **chicken wings**
  Milk
1 **tablespoon grated Parmesan cheese**
1 **tablespoon plain** *or* **Italian seasoned fine dry bread crumbs**
  Dash paprika

Remove the wing tips from the chicken; discard the tips. Separate the chicken wings at the joints. Dip the chicken pieces in milk. In a plastic bag combine the grated Parmesan cheese, fine dry bread crumbs, and paprika. Add the chicken pieces, one at a time; close the plastic bag and shake to coat. Place the coated chicken pieces in a 7-inch pie plate. Cover the chicken with waxed paper. Micro-cook, loosely covered, on 100% power for 3 to 5 minutes or till the chicken is tender, rotating the dish a half-turn every 2 minutes. Makes 1 or 2 appetizer servings.

ORANGE-CASHEW CHICKEN

⅓ **cup orange juice**
2 **tablespoons soy sauce**
½ **teaspoon grated gingerroot**
1 **whole large chicken breast, skinned, boned, and cut into bite-size pieces**
1 **teaspoon cooking oil**
1½ **teaspoons cornstarch**
1 **11-ounce can mandarin orange sections, drained**
2 **tablespoons cashews**
  Hot cooked rice

Stir together the orange juice, soy sauce, and grated gingerroot. Add the chicken pieces, stirring to coat. Let the chicken pieces stand in the orange juice mixture at room temperature for 30 minutes. Drain the chicken, reserving the orange juice mixture.

Preheat a 6½-inch microwave browning dish on 100% power for 3 minutes. Add the cooking oil. Swirl to coat the dish. Add the chicken pieces. Micro-cook, covered, on 100% power for 2 to 3 minutes or till tender, stirring every minute. Remove the chicken pieces, reserving the juices. Set the chicken aside.

Strain the cooking juices; return the juices to the browning dish. Stir together the reserved orange juice mixture and cornstarch. Stir into the cooking juices in the browning dish. Micro-cook, uncovered, on 100% power for 1 to 2 minutes or till the mixture is thickened and bubbly, stirring every 30 seconds. Stir in the chicken pieces, mandarin orange sections, and cashews. Micro-cook, uncovered, on 100% power about 30 seconds more or till heated through. Serve over hot cooked rice. Makes 2 servings.

CHICKEN ENCHILADAS

2 chicken thighs and 2 chicken backs
   (about 1 pound total)
½ cup water
2 tablespoons butter *or* margarine
2 tablespoons all-purpose flour
   Dash salt
   Dash paprika
   Dash crushed red pepper
   Dash pepper
⅔ cup milk
¼ cup shredded cheddar cheese (1 ounce)
2 tablespoons chopped canned green chili
   peppers
4 8-inch flour tortillas
¼ cup chili salsa
   Chili salsa
   Dairy sour cream

Place the chicken pieces in an 8x8x2-inch baking dish. Add water. Cover with vented clear plastic wrap. Micro-cook, covered, on 100% power for 8 to 10 minutes or till the chicken is tender, rotating the dish a half-turn after 5 minutes. Drain the chicken. When the chicken is cool enough to handle, remove the meat, discarding the bones and skin. Cut the chicken into bite-size pieces; set aside.

In a 4-cup measure micro-cook the butter or margarine, uncovered, on 100% power for 30 to 45 seconds or till melted. Stir in the flour, salt, paprika, crushed red pepper, and pepper. Stir in the milk. Micro-cook, uncovered, on 100% power for 1 to 2 minutes or till the mixture is thickened and bubbly, stirring every 30 seconds. Stir in the cheese and green chili peppers till the cheese is melted. Fold in the chicken.

Spoon the chicken-cheese mixture onto the tortillas; roll up the tortillas. Place the filled tortillas, seam side down, in the 8x8x2-inch baking dish. Cover with vented clear plastic wrap. Micro-cook, covered, on 70% power for 3 to 4 minutes or till heated through. Top the tortillas with the ¼ cup chili salsa; cover with vented clear plastic wrap. Micro-cook, covered, on 70% power about 1 minute more or till the salsa is heated through. Serve with additional chili salsa and dairy sour cream. Makes 2 servings.

BERRY-SAUCED CHICKEN DRUMSTICKS

2 chicken drumsticks
   Garlic salt
   Pepper
2 tablespoons red raspberry preserves
   or cherry preserves
1 tablespoon vinegar
½ teaspoon cornstarch
½ teaspoon soy sauce
⅛ teaspoon ground ginger

Place the chicken drumsticks in a 9-inch pie plate, with the meatiest portions to the outside of the dish. Sprinkle the drumsticks lightly with garlic salt and pepper. Cover the pie plate with waxed paper. Micro-cook, loosely covered, on 100% power for 3 to 4 minutes or till the chicken drumsticks are tender, rotating the dish a half-turn after 2 minutes. Drain off the fat. Let the chicken drumsticks stand, covered, while preparing the fruit sauce.

For the fruit sauce, in a 1-cup measure stir together red raspberry or cherry preserves, vinegar, cornstarch, soy sauce, and ground ginger. (Cut up any large pieces of fruit in the preserves, if necessary.) Micro-cook, uncovered, on 100% power about 1 minute or till the fruit sauce is thickened and bubbly, stirring once. Carefully spoon the fruit sauce over the chicken drumsticks. Micro-cook, loosely covered, on 100% power for 30 seconds to 1 minute more or till the chicken and the fruit sauce are heated through. Makes 1 serving.

Berry-Sauced Chicken Drumsticks for Two: The recipe for Berry-Sauced Chicken Drumsticks can be easily adapted for two people. Simply purchase 2 additional chicken drumsticks and double the remaining ingredients. Follow the original method, *except* micro-cook the 4 raw chicken drumsticks for 6 to 7 minutes, the sauce 45 seconds to 1 minute, and the chicken and sauce together for 1 to 1½ minutes.

CHEESE-PUFF FISH

½ of an 11½-ounce package (2 portions)
  frozen fish portions
2 tablespoons water
1 tablespoon butter *or* margarine
1 tablespoon all-purpose flour
⅛ teaspoon salt
⅛ teaspoon dried basil, crushed
  Dash pepper
¼ cup milk
¼ cup shredded Gruyère cheese (1 ounce)
¼ cup shredded carrot
1 egg yolk
1 egg white
  Dash cream of tartar

Place a frozen fish portion in each of two 10-ounce casseroles or au gratin dishes. Sprinkle *each* fish portion with *1 tablespoon* water. Cover with vented clear plastic wrap. Micro-cook, covered, on 30% power about 2 minutes or till fish is partially thawed, rotating the dishes a quarter-turn after 1 minute. Remove fish; use a sharp knife to cut the fish portions into ½-inch-thick slices. Return the fish slices to the 10-ounce casseroles or au gratin dishes. Cover with vented clear plastic wrap. Micro-cook, covered, on 100% power for 2 to 2½ minutes or till the fish is nearly done. Drain; set aside.

In a small nonmetal bowl micro-cook the butter or margarine, uncovered, on 100% power for 30 to 45 seconds or till melted. Stir in the flour, salt, basil, and pepper. Stir in the milk. Micro-cook, uncovered, on 100% power for 1 to 2 minutes or till the mixture is thickened and bubbly, stirring every 30 seconds. Stir in the shredded Gruyère cheese and shredded carrot till the cheese is melted.

With a fork or wire whisk beat the egg yolk slightly. Slowly add the cheese mixture to the beaten egg yolk, stirring constantly. Cool slightly. Using a rotary beater or electric mixer, beat the egg white and cream of tartar till stiff peaks form. Gently fold the beaten egg white into the cheese-egg yolk mixture. Spoon atop the fish slices in the casseroles or au gratin dishes. Micro-cook, uncovered, on 50% power for 6 to 8 minutes or just till egg mixture is set in the center, rotating each dish a half-turn every 2 minutes. Serve immediately. Makes 2 servings.

FISH CHOWDER

½ of an 11½-ounce package (2 portions)
  frozen fish portions
2 tablespoons water
1 slice bacon, cut into 1-inch pieces
1 stalk celery, bias sliced into ½-inch pieces
2 teaspoons sliced green onion
4 teaspoons all-purpose flour
⅛ teaspoon salt
⅛ teaspoon garlic powder
⅛ teaspoon dried thyme, crushed
1 cup milk
2 tablespoons dry white wine
½ teaspoon snipped parsley

Place the frozen fish portions in a 10x6x2-inch baking dish. Sprinkle water atop fish portions. Cover with vented clear plastic wrap. Micro-cook, covered, on 30% power about 2 minutes or till partially thawed, rotating the dish a quarter-turn after 1 minute. Use a sharp knife to cut the fish portions into bite-size pieces. Micro-cook, covered, on 100% power about 2 minutes more or till nearly done. Drain; set aside.

Place the bacon pieces in a 1-quart casserole. Cover with waxed paper. Micro-cook, loosely covered, on 100% power for 1½ to 2 minutes or till the bacon is done. Remove the bacon, reserving the drippings in the casserole. Crumble bacon; set aside.

Stir the celery and green onion into the bacon drippings in the casserole. Micro-cook, uncovered, on 100% power for 1½ to 2 minutes or till the vegetables are crisp-tender, stirring once. Stir in the flour, salt, garlic powder, and thyme. Stir in the milk. Micro-cook, uncovered, on 100% power about 3 minutes or till the mixture is thickened and bubbly, stirring every 30 seconds. Gently stir in fish pieces, wine, and parsley. Micro-cook, uncovered, on 100% power about 1 minute more or till heated through. Sprinkle with crumbled bacon. Makes 2 servings.

Substituting Frozen Green Beans: Frozen green beans come in a variety of forms that can often be substituted for each other. For example, the Hot Green Bean Salad and the Tuna-Green Bean Bake call for cut green beans, but you can substitute whole, French-style, or Italian green beans. If you substitute whole or Italian green beans, you may need to micro-cook them 1 to 2 minutes longer than you would micro-cook the cut green beans.

When choosing the type of frozen bean to use, keep in mind that whole green beans are the entire bean with string and ends removed, cut green beans are cut into 1-inch pieces, French-style green beans are sliced diagonally end to end, and Italian green beans look like flat green beans cut into 1-inch pieces.

When using a half-package of any frozen vegetable, as in the Hot Green Bean Salad or Tuna-Green Bean Bake, you can store the unused portion in your freezer. Simply seal the original container in a plastic bag or an airtight container.

TUNA-GREEN BEAN BAKE

½ of a 9-ounce package frozen
    cut green beans
1 tablespoon water
1 7½-ounce can semicondensed cream
    of mushroom soup
1 6½-ounce can tuna, drained and flaked,
    or one 5-ounce can chunk-style chicken,
    large pieces broken up
¼ cup sliced water chestnuts
1 tablespoon sliced green onion
1 tablespoon chopped pimiento
¼ teaspoon dried basil, crushed
⅓ cup chow mein noodles

In a 1-quart casserole combine the frozen green beans and water. Micro-cook, covered, on 100% power for 4 to 6 minutes or till the beans are tender, stirring once. Drain. Stir in the soup, tuna or chicken, sliced water chestnuts, sliced green onion, chopped pimiento, and basil. Micro-cook, uncovered, on 100% power for 2 to 3 minutes or till the mixture is heated through, stirring once. Sprinkle with the chow mein noodles. Micro-cook, uncovered, on 100% power for 1 minute more. Makes 2 servings.

HOT GREEN BEAN SALAD

½ of a 9-ounce package frozen
    cut green beans
1 tablespoon water
1 slice bacon, cut into 1-inch pieces
2 teaspoons sugar
½ teaspoon cornstarch
¼ teaspoon chili powder
    Dash salt
4 teaspoons water
2 teaspoons vinegar
4 cherry tomatoes, halved

In a 20-ounce casserole combine the frozen green beans and the 1 tablespoon water. Micro-cook, covered, on 100% power for 4 to 6 minutes or till the beans are tender, stirring once. Drain; set aside.

Place the bacon pieces in the same 20-ounce casserole. Cover with waxed paper. Micro-cook, loosely covered, on 100% power for 1 to 2 minutes or till the bacon is done. Remove the bacon, reserving 1 teaspoon of the drippings in the casserole. Crumble the bacon; set aside.

In a small bowl or custard cup combine the sugar, cornstarch, chili powder, and salt. Stir the sugar mixture into the reserved bacon drippings in the casserole. Add the 4 teaspoons water and the vinegar. Micro-cook, uncovered, on 100% power for 1 to 1½ minutes or till the mixture is thickened and bubbly, stirring every 30 seconds. Stir in the green beans and the cherry tomato halves. Micro-cook, uncovered, on 100% power for 1 to 1½ minutes or till heated through, stirring once. Sprinkle with crumbled bacon. Makes 2 servings.

RAISIN-SAUCED SQUASH

½ of a 1½-pound winter squash
   or one ¾-pound winter squash
¾ cup apricot nectar
1½ teaspoons cornstarch
⅛ teaspoon ground allspice
⅓ cup raisins

If using a whole squash, pierce the squash with a fork or a metal skewer several times, piercing all the way through to the center of the squash. Place the half or whole pierced squash in a 10x6x2-inch baking dish. Micro-cook, uncovered, on 100% power for 7 to 10 minutes or till the squash is tender, turning the squash once. Let stand 5 minutes.

Meanwhile, in a 2-cup measure stir together the apricot nectar, cornstarch, and ground allspice. Micro-cook, uncovered, on 100% power for 2 to 3 minutes or till the apricot mixture is thickened and bubbly, stirring every 30 seconds. Stir the raisins into the apricot mixture; set aside.

With one hand grasp the squash with a hot pad or towel. Use a sharp knife to cut the squash crosswise into 1-inch-thick slices; discard the seeds and stem ends. Return the squash slices to the baking dish. Pour the apricot-raisin mixture over the squash. Micro-cook, uncovered, on 100% power for 1 to 2 minutes or till heated through. Makes 2 servings.

WINTER SQUASH CUSTARDS

½ of a 1½-pound winter squash
   or one ¾-pound winter squash
1 beaten egg
2 tablespoons brown sugar
¼ teaspoon ground cinnamon
⅛ teaspoon ground cloves
½ cup milk
   Frozen whipped dessert topping, thawed

If using a whole squash, pierce the squash with a fork or metal skewer several times, piercing all the way through to the center. Place the half or whole squash in a 10x6x2-inch baking dish. Micro-cook, uncovered, on 100% power for 7 to 10 minutes or till the squash is tender, turning the squash once. Let stand 5 minutes.

If using a whole winter squash, grasp the squash with a hot pad or towel; cut the squash in half. Discard the seeds from cooked squash. Use a spoon to scoop out the pulp; mash the pulp (you should have ½ to ⅔ cup mashed pulp).

For the custard mixture, in a small mixing bowl combine the beaten egg, brown sugar, cinnamon, cloves, and mashed squash. Beat with a wire whisk or fork till combined. In a 2-cup measure micro-cook the milk, uncovered, on 100% power for 1 to 2 minutes or till very hot, but not boiling. Gradually add the hot milk to the squash mixture, beating constantly.

Spoon the custard mixture into two 6-ounce custard cups. Place the custard cups in the 10x6x2-inch baking dish. Pour ½ cup hot *water* into the baking dish around the custard cups. Cover with waxed paper. Micro-cook, loosely covered, on 50% power for 5 to 6 minutes, rotating the baking dish a quarter-turn every 2 minutes. Shake each custard gently to check doneness. Custards are done when slightly set but not firm. Remove custards as they are done. If necessary, continue to micro-cook, loosely covered, on 50% power for 1 to 2 minutes more, checking each custard for doneness every 15 seconds. Let stand for 10 minutes before serving. Serve with whipped dessert topping. Makes 2 dessert servings.

Types of Winter Squash: Winter squash is the common name used for mature, hard-shelled varieties of squash such as acorn, banana, butternut, turban, Hubbard, and buttercup squash. Acorn squash works well for the Winter Squash Custards and the Raisin-Sauced Squash, but you can use any winter squash variety for these versatile recipes.

•
Sit back and enjoy the simple pleasures of Raisin-Sauced Squash.

Micro-Cooking Spinach: To micro-cook leafy vegetables, such as spinach or collard greens, wash and trim the leaves. Do not pat the leaves dry because the water that clings to the greens adds moisture needed for micro-cooking.

SPINACH-YOGURT TOSS

½	of a 10-ounce package fresh spinach, stems removed (about 4 cups)
1	small clove garlic, halved
½	cup chopped sweet red *or* green pepper
1	teaspoon olive oil *or* cooking oil
3	tablespoons plain yogurt
¼	teaspoon dried mint, crushed
	Dash salt
	Dash ground turmeric
2	tablespoons broken walnuts
	Lemon wedges (optional)

Wash and tear the spinach leaves; *do not* pat dry. Place the spinach in a 20-ounce casserole. Micro-cook, covered, on 100% power for 1 to 1½ minutes or just till the spinach starts to wilt. Drain well. Rub a wooden salad bowl with the garlic; discard the garlic. Transfer the spinach to the wooden bowl.

In the same 20-ounce casserole combine the red or green pepper and the olive or cooking oil. Micro-cook, uncovered, on 100% power for 2 to 3 minutes or till the pepper is tender, stirring once. Stir in the plain yogurt, mint, salt, and ground turmeric. Spoon the yogurt mixture over the wilted spinach in the bowl; toss gently till the spinach is well coated. Cover and chill for several hours. Before serving, sprinkle with the broken walnuts. Garnish with lemon wedges, if desired. Makes 2 servings.

CREAMY DILLED SPINACH

½	of a 10-ounce package fresh spinach, stems removed (about 4 cups)
3	tablespoons finely chopped onion
1	tablespoon butter *or* margarine
2	teaspoons all-purpose flour
⅛	teaspoon salt
	Dash ground nutmeg
	Dash pepper
⅓	cup chicken broth
¼	cup dairy sour cream
1	teaspoon all-purpose flour
¼	teaspoon dried dillweed

Wash and tear the spinach leaves; *do not* pat dry. Place the spinach in a 1½-quart casserole; cover with vented clear plastic wrap. Micro-cook, covered, on 100% power for 2 to 3 minutes or till the spinach is done, stirring once. Drain well.

In a 2-cup measure micro-cook the onion and butter or margarine, uncovered, on 100% power for 1 to 2 minutes or till the onion is tender. Stir in the 2 teaspoons flour, salt, nutmeg, and pepper. Stir in the chicken broth. Micro-cook, uncovered, on 100% power for 1 to 2 minutes or till the mixture is thickened and bubbly, stirring every 30 seconds. Stir into the spinach. Combine sour cream, the 1 teaspoon flour, and dillweed. Stir into spinach mixture. Micro-cook, uncovered, on 100% power about 1 minute or till heated through. Makes 2 servings.

SHERRIED MUSHROOMS AND ZUCCHINI

  1 small zucchini, cut into 2-inch julienne strips
  2 tablespoons water
  ¼ of a 1-pound package fresh
       mushrooms, sliced (about 1½ cups)
  2 teaspoons butter *or* margarine
  1 teaspoon dry sherry
  ⅛ teaspoon salt
  ⅛ teaspoon celery seed

In a 1-quart casserole combine the zucchini and the water. Micro-cook, covered, on 100% power for 2 minutes, stirring once. Stir in the sliced mushrooms. Micro-cook, covered, on 100% power for 2 to 3 minutes more or till the zucchini and mushrooms are tender, stirring once. Drain off the liquid. Add the butter or margarine, sherry, salt, and celery seed; toss gently till the butter or margarine is melted and the vegetables are coated. Makes 2 servings.

MUSHROOMS AU GRATIN

  ½ of a 1-pound package fresh mushrooms,
       halved (about 3 cups)
  2 teaspoons butter *or* margarine
  1 tablespoon all-purpose flour
       Dash salt
       Dash pepper
       Pinch dried thyme, crushed
  ¼ cup milk
  ½ cup shredded American cheese (2 ounces)
  2 teaspoons snipped parsley
  ¼ cup croutons, coarsely crushed

In a 20-ounce casserole combine the mushrooms and butter or margarine. Cover with vented clear plastic wrap. Micro-cook, covered, on 100% power for 2 to 3 minutes or till the mushrooms are tender, stirring once.

Stir in the flour, salt, pepper, and thyme. Stir in the milk. Micro-cook, uncovered, on 100% power for 2 to 3 minutes or till the mixture is thickened and bubbly, stirring every 30 seconds. Add the shredded American cheese and snipped parsley; stir till the cheese is melted. Sprinkle the crushed croutons atop the mushroom-cheese mixture. Micro-cook, uncovered, on 100% power for 1 to 2 minutes or till heated through. Makes 2 servings.

MARINATED MUSHROOM SALAD

  ¼ of a 1-pound package fresh
       mushrooms, sliced (about 1½ cups)
  ¾ cup water
  1 large green onion, bias sliced into
       ½-inch pieces
  3 tablespoons salad oil
  2 tablespoons red wine vinegar
  1 teaspoon prepared mustard
  ¼ teaspoon dried thyme, crushed
       Dash freshly ground black pepper
       Bibb *or* leaf lettuce leaves
       Snipped parsley

In a 1-quart casserole combine the sliced mushrooms, water, and bias-sliced green onion. Micro-cook, covered, on 100% power for 3 to 4 minutes or just till tender, stirring once. Drain.

In a screw-top jar combine the salad oil, red wine vinegar, mustard, thyme, and pepper. Cover; shake well. Pour the oil-vinegar mixture over the vegetables. Cover; chill at least 2 hours. Drain the vegetables. Arrange the vegetables on lettuce leaves; sprinkle with snipped parsley. Makes 1 serving.

Marinated Mushroom Salad for Two: An easy way to stretch the Marinated Mushroom Salad to make two servings is to simply add torn greens. Fresh spinach or red leaf lettuce is a nice addition to this recipe and should be tossed with the marinated vegetables just before serving.

When selecting the mushrooms for the Marinated Mushroom Salad or any of the recipes on this page, the freshness and shape of the mushrooms should be the first considerations. Look for mushroom caps that are closed around the stem and not wilted. The color of mushrooms depends on the variety, but the most common colors are white, off-white, and tan.

When preparing the mushrooms for these recipes, rinse them gently in cold water and pat dry with a towel. To store mushrooms that aren't used right away, refrigerate them in their original covered container or in a plastic bag for up to two days.

Frozen Broccoli

CHEESY BROCCOLI SOUP

½ of a 10-ounce package frozen
    chopped broccoli
½ cup thinly sliced carrot
½ cup water
1 teaspoon instant chicken bouillon granules
1 cup milk
½ cup shredded American cheese (2 ounces)
½ cup chopped cooked chicken *or*
    finely chopped fully cooked ham
⅛ teaspoon pepper
¼ cup water
2 tablespoons all-purpose flour

In a 1-quart casserole combine the frozen chopped broccoli, thinly sliced carrot, the ½ cup water, and instant chicken bouillon granules. Micro-cook, covered, on 100% power for 5 to 7 minutes or till the vegetables are tender, stirring once.

To the vegetables in the 1-quart casserole, stir in the milk, shredded American cheese, chopped chicken or finely chopped ham, and pepper. In a small bowl stir together the ¼ cup water and flour; stir into the vegetable-cheese mixture in the casserole. Micro-cook, uncovered, on 100% power about 5 minutes or till the mixture is thickened and bubbly, stirring every minute. Micro-cook, uncovered, on 100% power for 30 seconds more. Makes 2 servings.

BROCCOLI-VEGETABLE DIP

½ of a 10-ounce package frozen
    chopped broccoli
1 tablespoon water
1 3-ounce package cream cheese
    with chives, softened
1 teaspoon milk
½ teaspoon Worcestershire sauce
    Dash pepper
    Dash bottled hot pepper sauce
    Assorted fresh vegetable dippers such as
    carrot sticks, cauliflower flowerets,
    celery sticks, cherry tomatoes,
    cucumber slices, green pepper strips, *or*
    zucchini slices

In a 1-quart casserole combine the frozen chopped broccoli and the water. Micro-cook, covered, on 100% power for 3 to 5 minutes or till the broccoli is tender, stirring once. Drain. Cut up any large pieces of broccoli; set aside.

In a small mixer bowl combine the softened cream cheese with chives, the milk, Worcestershire sauce, pepper, and bottled hot pepper sauce. Beat the cream cheese mixture on medium speed of an electric mixer till smooth. Add the cooked, drained broccoli to the cream cheese mixture. Continue beating on medium speed of electric mixer till the cream cheese-broccoli mixture is well combined. Serve with assorted fresh vegetable dippers. Makes 2 servings.

A crock of Cheesy Broccoli Soup is the perfect choice for lunch on an activity-filled day.

RASPBERRY-ORANGE TART

Pastry for a 4½-inch Pie Shell
½ of a 10-ounce package frozen red
raspberries, thawed
2 tablespoons sugar
2 teaspoons cornstarch
⅛ teaspoon ground cinnamon
1 small orange, peeled and sectioned
Vanilla Custard Sauce (optional)

Prepare and micro-cook Pastry for a 4½-inch Pie Shell. Mash the *undrained* raspberries in a small non-metal bowl. Combine the sugar, cornstarch, and cinnamon; stir into the mashed raspberries. Micro-cook, uncovered, on 100% power for 2 to 2½ minutes or till the mixture is thickened and bubbly, stirring every 30 seconds. Gently fold in the orange sections. Spoon the raspberry-orange mixture into the pastry shell. Cover and chill for at least 2 hours. Pour Vanilla Custard Sauce around tart, if desired. Makes 2 servings.

Pastry for a 4½-inch Pie Shell

In a small mixing bowl stir together ½ cup all-purpose *flour*, ¼ teaspoon *salt*, and dash ground *cinnamon*; cut in 3 tablespoons *shortening or lard* till pieces are the size of small peas. Sprinkle 1 tablespoon *cold water* over the mixture. Gently toss with a fork and push moistened portion to side of bowl. Repeat, if necessary, tossing the mixture with 1 to 2 teaspoons more *cold water* to moisten.

Gather up the dough; form into a ball. On a lightly floured surface flatten the ball slightly with your hands. Roll the dough from center to edge into a 7-inch circle. Ease the dough into a 4½-inch quiche dish or pie plate, being careful to avoid stretching the dough. Flute the edges high. Prick with tines of a fork at ½-inch intervals. Micro-cook, uncovered, on 100% power for 3 to 5 minutes or till the crust is dry, rotating the dish a quarter-turn every minute.

Vanilla Custard Sauce

In a 2-cup measure stir together 1 beaten *egg yolk*, 3 tablespoons *sugar*, 1 tablespoon softened *butter or margarine*, and 1 teaspoon *cornstarch*. Stir in ⅔ cup *milk*. Micro-cook, uncovered, on 100% power for 1½ to 2 minutes or till thickened and bubbly, stirring every 30 seconds. Stir in ½ teaspoon *vanilla*.

RASPBERRY-SAUCED CHEESECAKE

1 tablespoon butter *or* margarine
⅓ cup finely crushed graham crackers
2 teaspoons sugar
1 3-ounce package cream cheese
¼ cup dairy sour cream
3 tablespoons sugar
¼ teaspoon vanilla
1 egg
1 tablespoon sugar
1½ teaspoons cornstarch
½ of a 10-ounce package frozen red
raspberries, thawed

For the crust, in a 15-ounce casserole or custard cup micro-cook the butter or margarine, uncovered, on 100% power for 30 to 45 seconds or till melted. Stir in crushed crackers and the 2 teaspoons sugar. Press the mixture firmly against the bottom and 1½ inches up the side of the casserole or custard cup to form a crust. Micro-cook, uncovered, on 100% power for 30 seconds to 1 minute or till set, rotating the casserole or custard cup a half-turn after 20 seconds.

For the filling, unwrap the cream cheese and place in a nonmetal mixing bowl. Micro-cook, uncovered, on 50% power for 45 seconds to 1 minute or till softened. Stir in sour cream, 3 tablespoons sugar, and vanilla. Add the egg, beating just till combined. Pour the filling into the prepared crust. Micro-cook, uncovered, on 50% power for 4 to 5 minutes or just till the mixture appears set, giving the casserole or custard cup a quarter-turn every minute. (When done, the center will be slightly set but not firm.) Cool; chill at least 2 hours.

For the sauce, in a small nonmetal bowl or 2-cup measure stir together the 1 tablespoon sugar and cornstarch. Stir in the *undrained* raspberries. Micro-cook, uncovered, on 100% power for 1 to 2 minutes or till the mixture is thickened and bubbly, stirring every 30 seconds. Sieve the mixture, discarding seeds. Cool slightly. Serve the warm sauce with the cheesecake. Makes 2 servings.

The delectable flavor and appearance of Raspberry-Orange Tart are sure to get a standing ovation time after time.

HOT FRUIT MEDLEY

¼ of a medium pineapple, peeled and cut into
    chunks (about 1 cup), *or* one 8¼-ounce
    can pineapple chunks, drained
½ cup fresh raspberries
½ cup fresh blueberries
3 tablespoons orange liqueur
2 tablespoons brown sugar
1 tablespoon butter *or* margarine
    Dash ground cinnamon
    Dash ground allspice
    Dairy sour cream *or* plain yogurt (optional)

In a 20-ounce casserole stir together pineapple, raspberries, blueberries, orange liqueur, brown sugar, butter or margarine, cinnamon, and allspice. Micro-cook, uncovered, on 100% power for 3 to 4 minutes or till heated through, stirring twice. Serve warm with sour cream or yogurt, if desired. Makes 2 servings.

FROZEN PINEAPPLE PARFAITS

⅛ of a medium pineapple, peeled and
    chopped (about ½ cup), *or* ½ of an
    8-ounce can crushed pineapple, drained
1 tablespoon sugar
⅛ teaspoon ground cinnamon
2 teaspoons butter *or* margarine
⅓ cup crushed granola
1 cup pineapple *or* orange sherbet, softened

In a small nonmetal bowl micro-cook the pineapple, uncovered, on 100% power for 3 minutes, stirring once. Stir in sugar and cinnamon. Micro-cook, uncovered, on 100% power for 1 to 2 minutes or till sugar is dissolved, stirring every minute. Chill thoroughly.

In a custard cup or small nonmetal bowl micro-cook butter or margarine, uncovered, on 100% power for 30 to 45 seconds or till melted. Stir in granola. Line two 6-ounce custard cups with clear plastic wrap. Spoon ¼ *cup* of the sherbet evenly into *each* of the custard cups. Top the sherbet in *each* custard cup with *one-fourth* of the pineapple mixture and *one-fourth* of the granola mixture. Place the custard cups in the freezer for 15 minutes. Remove from freezer; repeat layers of sherbet, pineapple mixture, and granola mixture. Return the custard cups to the freezer; freeze several hours or till firm. Remove from freezer and let stand 5 minutes before serving. Unmold by inverting the custard cups onto a serving plate; remove plastic wrap. Makes 2 servings.

PINEAPPLE CRISP

2 tablespoons quick-cooking rolled oats
2 tablespoons brown sugar
1 tablespoon all-purpose flour
    Dash ground cinnamon
    Dash ground nutmeg
1 tablespoon butter *or* margarine
¼ of a medium pineapple, peeled and cut into
    chunks (about 1 cup), *or* one 8¼-ounce
    can pineapple chunks, drained
    Vanilla ice cream (optional)

Stir together rolled oats, brown sugar, flour, cinnamon, and nutmeg. Cut in the butter or margarine till mixture resembles coarse crumbs. Place pineapple in a 10-ounce casserole or custard cup. Sprinkle the rolled oats mixture atop the pineapple. Micro-cook, uncovered, on 100% power for 2 to 4 minutes or till the pineapple is heated through, rotating the casserole a quarter-turn every minute. Serve warm with vanilla ice cream, if desired. Makes 1 serving.

PIÑA COLADA FRUIT DISH

¼ cup sugar
1 tablespoon cornstarch
⅔ cup unsweetened pineapple juice
2 tablespoons coconut liqueur
⅜ of a medium pineapple, peeled and cut into
    chunks (about 1½ cups), *or* 1½ cups
    drained, canned pineapple chunks
¼ cup coconut, toasted

In a 2-cup measure combine sugar and cornstarch. Stir in pineapple juice. Micro-cook, uncovered, on 100% power for 1 to 2 minutes or till thickened and bubbly, stirring every 30 seconds. Stir in liqueur. Stir into pineapple chunks. Cover and chill several hours or overnight. Serve in individual dessert dishes. Sprinkle with coconut before serving. Makes 2 servings.

• **Dividing Pineapple and Removing the Core:** After removing the crown from the pineapple (see the tip below), use a long, sharp knife to cut the pineapple lengthwise into sections. When dividing the pineapple into sections for the recipes on page 78, it is best to cut the fruit into either four or eight sections.

To remove the hard center core from each pineapple section, begin at one end and cut underneath the core. Cut away from yourself and cut only until you reach the center, as shown in the photo. Then turn the pineapple section around and, starting at the other end, cut away from yourself back to the center; remove the core.

Selecting Pineapple and Removing the Crown: Because pineapple does not ripen after harvesting, choose one that is at the peak of ripeness and flavor. The pineapple you choose should be plump, slightly soft to the touch, heavy for its size, and have a fragrant pineapple odor. When fully ripe, pineapple is golden yellow, orange-yellow, or reddish brown, depending on the variety you choose.

To remove the leafy crown on the top part of the pineapple, grasp pineapple with one hand and crown with the other; twist in opposite directions. Use a towel or pot holder to protect your hands from the sharp sides and the top of the fruit, if necessary.

The sooner you use a pineapple after purchase, the better it will be. Holding at room temperature causes softening and acid loss, but will not cause the fruit to ripen. You may store the whole pineapple or the pineapple sections in the refrigerator for one to two days.

Removing the Peel of the Pineapple: Use a long, sharp knife to cut along the underside of each pineapple section to remove the tough outer covering, as shown in the photo.

• **Cutting Out the "Eyes" of the Pineapple:** After removing the pineapple peel, turn the fruit over and use a paring knife to carefully cut out any dark "eyes" on the fruit.

Dividing the Gingerbread Mix: When dividing the 14½-ounce package of gingerbread mix into four portions for the recipes on pages 80 and 81, use this tip to get an equal amount of mix for each recipe. Measure the entire package of gingerbread mix and divide it into fourths all at once, rather than spooning out a rough measure from the package each time you make one of the recipes. You can seal the individual portions of gingerbread mix in plastic bags or airtight containers and store them till needed.

APPLE GINGERBREAD

> 1 medium cooking apple, peeled and sliced
> ¼ cup sugar
> 2 teaspoons all-purpose flour
> 1 teaspoon lemon juice
> 2 tablespoons semisweet chocolate pieces (optional)
> ¼ of a 14½-ounce package (about ⅔ cup) gingerbread mix
> ¼ cup warm water

In a 20-ounce casserole toss together the apple, sugar, flour, and lemon juice. Micro-cook, covered, on 100% power for 2 to 3 minutes or till the apple slices are tender, stirring every minute. Stir in the semisweet chocolate pieces, if desired.

In a small bowl stir together the gingerbread mix and warm water. Spoon the batter atop the apple mixture in the casserole. Micro-cook, uncovered, on 50% power for 4 to 5 minutes or till done, rotating the casserole a quarter-turn every minute. (When done, the surface may still appear moist but a wooden pick inserted into the center should come out clean.) Serve warm. Makes 2 servings.

GINGERBREAD-CARROT CUPCAKES

> ¼ of a 14½-ounce package (about ⅔ cup) gingerbread mix
> ½ cup shredded carrot
> ¼ cup warm water
> ¼ of a 3-ounce package cream cheese, softened
> ¼ teaspoon vanilla
> ½ cup sifted powdered sugar
> ½ to 1 teaspoon milk

For the cupcakes, in a small mixing bowl stir together the gingerbread mix, shredded carrot, and warm water. Line four 6-ounce custard cups or a microwave cupcake dish with paper bake cups. Fill the cups ⅔ full. Micro-cook, uncovered, on 100% power for 1½ to 2½ minutes or till the cupcakes are done, rotating the custard cups or the cupcake dish a quarter-turn every minute. (When done, the surface may still appear moist, but a wooden pick inserted into the center should come out clean.) Remove the cupcakes to a wire rack to cool.

For the frosting, in a small mixer bowl beat together the softened cream cheese and vanilla till light and fluffy. Gradually add the powdered sugar, beating till smooth. Beat in enough milk to make the mixture of spreading consistency. Frost the cupcakes with the cream cheese frosting. Makes 4 cupcakes.

CRANBERRY GINGERBREAD DESSERT

¼ of a 14½-ounce package (about ⅔ cup)
  gingerbread mix
¼ cup warm water
⅓ cup coarsely chopped cranberries
2 tablespoons chopped walnuts

In a small mixing bowl stir together the gingerbread mix and water. Add the chopped cranberries and nuts; mix well. Turn the batter into a lightly greased 15-ounce casserole or custard cup. Micro-cook, uncovered, on 50% power for 4 to 5 minutes or till done, rotating the casserole or custard cup a quarter-turn twice. (When done, the surface may still appear moist, but a wooden pick inserted into the center should come out clean.) Let stand in the casserole or custard cup for 5 minutes. Invert the casserole onto a wire rack; let cool about 5 minutes more. Serve warm. Makes 2 servings.

Storing Fresh Cranberries: Fresh cranberries are perennial holiday favorites, but because they store so well you can enjoy their tart flavor any time of the year. Use the cranberries you'll need for the Cranberry Gingerbread Dessert, then store the rest in the refrigerator in their original package or loosely covered for up to two months. Or, for longer storage you can freeze cranberries by wrapping the unused portion in moisture-vaporproof material. Place the sealed and labeled package in the freezer and store it for up to one year. Be sure to rinse and sort fresh or frozen cranberries before using.

GINGERBREAD WITH LEMON SAUCE

¼ of a 14½-ounce package (about ⅔ cup)
  gingerbread mix
¼ cup warm water
¼ cup sugar
2 teaspoons cornstarch
¼ cup water
¼ teaspoon finely shredded lemon peel
1 tablespoon lemon juice
1 tablespoon butter *or* margarine

In a small mixing bowl stir together the gingerbread mix and ¼ cup warm water. Turn the batter into a lightly greased 15-ounce casserole or custard cup. Micro-cook, uncovered, on 50% power for 3 to 4 minutes or till done, rotating the casserole or custard cup a quarter-turn every minute. (When done, the surface may still appear moist, but a wooden pick inserted into the center should come out clean.) Let stand while preparing the lemon sauce.

For the lemon sauce, in a 1-cup measure stir together sugar and cornstarch. Stir in ¼ cup water, lemon peel, and lemon juice. Micro-cook, uncovered, on 100% power for 1 to 1½ minutes or till the mixture is thickened and bubbly, stirring every 30 seconds. Stir in the butter or margarine till melted. Serve the warm lemon sauce atop gingerbread. Makes 2 servings.

ONE-DISH MEALS

One-dish meals are nearly every cook's favorites because they are so easy to prepare and to serve. This chapter features several delicious one- or two-serving micro-cooked dishes, such as *Lamb and Vegetable Combo*, that can be the meal's mainstay (see recipe, page 90). For most of these dishes, a salad, dessert, beverage, and perhaps a bread are all you'll need to make the meal complete.

Micro-Cooking Chicken: When a recipe such as Herbed Chicken and Dumplings calls for cooked chicken, you can use your microwave oven to cook the chicken quickly. Just start with a 1-pound whole chicken breast with the skin and bones intact. Place the chicken breast in a 1½-quart casserole. Add 1 tablespoon water. Micro-cook, covered, on 100% power for 4 minutes. Turn the chicken breast over and micro-cook, covered, on 100% power for 2 to 3 minutes more or till the chicken is done. Drain and cool the chicken. With a sharp knife, cut the chicken meat away from the bones and into cubes. Makes 1 cup of cubed, cooked chicken.

HERBED CHICKEN AND DUMPLINGS

- ¾ cup frozen peas and carrots
- 2 tablespoons butter *or* margarine
- 2 tablespoons all-purpose flour
- ¼ teaspoon dried marjoram, crushed
  Dash pepper
- ⅔ cup chicken broth
- ⅓ cup milk
- 1 cup cubed, cooked chicken
- ½ cup packaged biscuit mix
- 2 tablespoons milk
- 1 teaspoon dried parsley flakes
- ¼ cup shredded cheddar cheese *or* Swiss cheese (1 ounce)

In a 1-quart casserole micro-cook frozen peas and carrots in butter or margarine, covered, on 100% power about 3 minutes or till vegetables are crisp-tender, stirring once. Stir in flour, marjoram, and pepper. Stir in chicken broth and the ⅓ cup milk. Micro-cook, uncovered, on 100% power about 4 minutes or till the mixture is thickened and bubbly, stirring every minute. Stir in the chicken. Micro-cook, uncovered, on 100% power about 1 minute more or till the chicken is heated through.

Meanwhile, stir together biscuit mix, the 2 tablespoons milk, and dried parsley. Drop in 4 mounds atop the hot chicken mixture. Micro-cook, uncovered, on 50% power for 5 to 6 minutes more or till dumplings are just set. Sprinkle with cheese. Micro-cook, uncovered, on 100% power for 45 seconds to 1 minute or till cheese is melted. Makes 2 servings.

SCALLOP MÉLANGE

- ½ pound fresh *or* frozen scallops
- 2 stalks celery, bias sliced into ½-inch pieces
- ½ of a medium sweet red *or* green pepper, cut into ¾-inch squares
- 2 teaspoons cornstarch
- ¼ teaspoon salt
- ⅛ teaspoon dried basil, crushed
  Dash pepper
- ⅔ cup milk
- 1 cup cooked rice
- ½ cup shredded Swiss cheese (2 ounces)
- 1 tablespoon dry white wine
  Celery leaves (optional)

Thaw scallops, if frozen. (To thaw scallops in the microwave oven, place the frozen scallops in a 1½-quart casserole. Micro-cook, covered, on 30% power for 2 to 4 minutes or just till thawed, stirring every minute.) Use a sharp knife to halve any large scallops.

In a 1½-quart casserole combine the fresh or thawed scallops, celery pieces, and pepper squares. Micro-cook, covered, on 100% power for 4 to 5 minutes or till the scallops are nearly done, stirring once. Drain in a colander and set aside.

In the same 1½-quart casserole combine the cornstarch, salt, dried basil, and pepper. Stir in the milk. Micro-cook, uncovered, on 100% power for 1½ to 2 minutes or till the mixture is thickened and bubbly, stirring every minute.

Gently stir in the cooked rice, shredded Swiss cheese, dry white wine, and the cooked scallops and vegetables. Spoon the scallop-rice mixture into two 15-ounce casseroles. Micro-cook, uncovered, on 100% power about 1 minute more or till heated through, rearranging the casseroles once. Garnish with celery leaves, if desired. Makes 2 servings.

SWEET-SOUR BEEF 'N' CABBAGE

½ of a small head cabbage
¼ cup water
½ pound ground beef
2 tablespoons chopped onion
2 tablespoons sliced celery
2 teaspoons all-purpose flour
¼ teaspoon garlic salt
  Dash pepper
1 8-ounce can tomato sauce
2 tablespoons vinegar
1 tablespoon brown sugar

Cut the half head of cabbage into 4 wedges. Carefully cut off most of the core from each wedge, leaving some of the core to help hold the wedges together. Place the wedges in a 1-quart casserole; sprinkle with water. Micro-cook, covered, on 100% power for 10 to 12 minutes or till the cabbage wedges are tender, rearranging the cabbage wedges once during cooking. Drain off the water; cover the cabbage wedges and set aside.

Crumble the ground beef into a 10x6x2-inch baking dish. Stir in the chopped onion and sliced celery. Micro-cook, uncovered, on 100% power for 2 to 3 minutes or till the meat is no longer pink, stirring once to break up the meat. Drain off the fat. Stir in the flour, garlic salt, and pepper. Stir together the tomato sauce, vinegar, and brown sugar. Add the tomato mixture to the ground beef mixture; mix well. Micro-cook, uncovered, on 100% power for 3 to 5 minutes or till the ground beef mixture is heated through. To serve, transfer the cooked cabbage wedges to a serving platter. Spoon the ground beef mixture over the cabbage wedges. Makes 2 servings.

Selecting and Coring Cabbage: When it comes time for you to choose the cabbage for Sweet-Sour Beef 'n' Cabbage, look for a firm cabbage head that is heavy for its size. The outer leaves of the cabbage should be a rich green color, reasonably crisp, and free of blemishes.

Before you cook the cabbage, you must remove the tough core. To remove the core, cut the half head of cabbage into wedges. Carefully cut off most of the core from each wedge, leaving some of the core to help hold the wedge together. You can discard the core and outer leaves or save them and use them later in a soup stock.

HAMBURGER PIE

½ pound ground beef
2 tablespoons chopped onion
1 8-ounce can cut green beans, drained
½ of a 15-ounce can (about 1 cup)
  tomato herb sauce
  Dash pepper
2 small potatoes, peeled and cubed, *or* 1 large
  potato, peeled and cubed
2 tablespoons water
  Milk
¼ cup shredded cheddar cheese (1 ounce)

Crumble the ground beef into a 1-quart casserole. Stir in the chopped onion. Micro-cook, uncovered, on 100% power for 2 to 3 minutes or till the meat is no longer pink, stirring once to break up the meat. Drain off the fat. Stir in the green beans, tomato herb sauce, and pepper; set aside.

Place the potato cubes in a medium nonmetal bowl. Sprinkle with water. Cover with vented clear plastic wrap. Micro-cook, covered, on 100% power for 6 to 8 minutes or till tender. Drain. Mash the potatoes while they are still hot. Add enough milk (1 to 3 tablespoons) to make potatoes fluffy, yet stiff enough to hold their shape. Season potatoes lightly with salt and pepper.

Return the ground beef mixture to the microwave oven. Micro-cook, uncovered, on 100% power for 2 to 4 minutes or till heated through, stirring once. Spoon the mashed potatoes into mounds atop the hot meat mixture. Sprinkle the shredded cheddar cheese atop the mounds of mashed potato. Micro-cook, uncovered, on 100% power for 1½ to 2 minutes or till the cheese is melted. Makes 2 servings.

TAMALE PIE

½ pound bulk Italian sausage
½ of a small onion, sliced and separated into rings
2 tablespoons chopped canned green chili peppers
2 teaspoons all-purpose flour
1 7½-ounce can tomatoes, cut up
¼ cup all-purpose flour
¼ cup yellow cornmeal
2 teaspoons sugar
1 teaspoon baking powder
¼ teaspoon salt
1 beaten egg
2 tablespoons milk
2 tablespoons chopped canned green chili peppers
1 tablespoon cooking oil
2 tablespoons shredded cheddar cheese

Crumble Italian sausage into a 1-quart casserole. Stir in the onion. Micro-cook, uncovered, on 100% power for 2 to 3 minutes or till the meat is done, stirring once to break up the meat. Drain off the fat. Stir in 2 tablespoons chili peppers and the 2 teaspoons flour. Stir in the *undrained* tomatoes. Micro-cook, uncovered, on 100% power for 2 to 3 minutes or till slightly thickened and bubbly, stirring every minute. Micro-cook, uncovered, on 100% power for 30 seconds more.

Meanwhile, stir together the ¼ cup all-purpose flour, cornmeal, sugar, baking powder, and salt. Combine the egg, milk, 2 tablespoons chili peppers, and cooking oil. Stir into the flour mixture just till moistened (do not overbeat). Spread atop the hot meat mixture. Micro-cook, uncovered, on 50% power for 2 to 4 minutes or till the topping is nearly set, rotating the dish a quarter-turn every minute. Sprinkle with the shredded cheddar cheese. Micro-cook, uncovered, on 100% power about 30 seconds more or till the cheese is melted. Makes 2 servings.

• Teenagers especially love the south-of-the-border flavor in our microwave version of Tamale Pie.

TACO-TOPPED POTATO

1 medium baking potato
¼ pound ground beef
1 tablespoon chopped onion
¼ cup taco sauce
¼ teaspoon Worcestershire sauce
2 tablespoons shredded cheddar cheese
Dairy sour cream

Wash and prick potato. Place in a shallow baking dish. Micro-cook, uncovered, on 100% power for 3 to 5 minutes or till nearly tender. Let stand for 5 minutes.

Meanwhile, in a small baking dish crumble ground beef. Stir in onion. Micro-cook, uncovered, on 100% power for 2 to 3 minutes or till the meat is no longer pink, stirring once to break up meat. Drain off fat. Stir in the taco sauce and Worcestershire sauce. Micro-cook, uncovered, on 100% power for 1 to 1½ minutes more or till heated through.

Cut the potato in half lengthwise; slightly mash. Top with ground beef mixture and shredded cheddar cheese. Dollop with sour cream. Makes 1 serving.

SAUSAGE-STUFFED SQUASH

1 medium acorn squash
½ pound bulk pork sausage
2 tablespoons chopped onion
½ cup cornbread stuffing mix
1 tablespoon water
¼ cup shredded Monterey Jack cheese

Pierce whole squash with a metal skewer several times, piercing all the way through to the center. Place the squash in a shallow baking dish. Micro-cook, uncovered, on 100% power for 6 to 8 minutes or till tender, turning squash over once. Set aside.

Crumble the sausage into a 1-quart casserole. Stir in the chopped onion. Micro-cook, uncovered, on 100% power for 3 to 4 minutes or till the sausage is no longer pink. Drain off the fat.

Stir stuffing mix and water into sausage mixture. With one hand grasp the squash with a hot pad or towel. Halve the squash lengthwise; discard the seeds. Scrape out the pulp, leaving shells; mash pulp with a fork. Stir into sausage-stuffing mixture. Spoon into squash shells. Micro-cook, covered, on 100% power for 3 to 4 minutes or till heated through. Sprinkle with the shredded Monterey Jack cheese. Micro-cook, uncovered, on 100% power for 30 to 45 seconds or till the cheese is melted. Makes 2 servings.

KNACKWURST AND POTATO SALAD

½ pound tiny new potatoes
2 tablespoons water
2 slices bacon, cut into ½-inch pieces
2 stalks celery, bias sliced into
    ½-inch pieces
2 tablespoons chopped onion
1½ teaspoons all-purpose flour
1½ teaspoons sugar
¼ teaspoon celery seed
  Dash pepper
¼ cup water
2 tablespoons vinegar
1 hard-cooked egg, sliced
2 4-inch links fully cooked knackwurst *or*
    Polish sausage

Use a potato peeler or sharp knife to peel a strip around the center of each potato. Place the potatoes in a circle in a 7-inch pie plate; sprinkle with the 2 tablespoons water. Micro-cook, covered, on 100% power for 3 to 4 minutes or till the potatoes are tender, rotating the pie plate a half-turn once. Drain. Let the potatoes stand, covered, while preparing dressing.

For the dressing, in a 4-cup measure micro-cook the bacon, loosely covered, on 100% power for 1 to 1½ minutes or till nearly done. Add the sliced celery and chopped onion to the bacon. Micro-cook, covered, on 100% power for 1½ to 2 minutes or till the celery and onion are tender, stirring once. Stir in the flour, sugar, celery seed, and pepper. Add the ¼ cup water and the vinegar; mix well.

Micro-cook, uncovered, on 100% power for 1½ to 2 minutes or till the mixture is thickened and bubbly, stirring every 30 seconds. Gently toss together the dressing, potatoes, and egg slices. Spoon the potato mixture into the center of the 7-inch pie plate.

Cut deep slits 1 inch apart in each sausage link, cutting to, but not through, the opposite side. Place the sausage links on a nonmetal plate or shallow baking dish. Micro-cook, uncovered, on 100% power for 1 minute to remove excess fat from the sausage. Drain on paper toweling. Carefully place the sausage links, with the cut edges of the sausage to the outside, around the outer edge of the potato mixture. Micro-cook, uncovered, on 100% power for 1 to 2 minutes or till heated through. Makes 2 servings.

Slitting the Sausages: To help vent steam and rid the meat of excess fat during micro-cooking, cut slits in the knackwurst or Polish sausage with a sharp knife. The slits also cause the sausage links to curve slightly and fit attractively around the edge of the dish. To make the slits, cut deep slashes about 1 inch apart in the meat. Cut to, but not through, the opposite side of each sausage link. When you're ready to add the sausage links to the pie plate, place them around the potato mixture. Position the sausages so the cut edges are to the outside and curve them so they fit against the edge of the dish.

Micro-Cooking Potatoes: Some vegetables with a skin, such as potatoes, need to vent steam during micro-cooking. Usually you use a fork or a sharp knife to prick the vegetables. In the case of Knackwurst and Potato Salad, however, you peel a strip from around the center of each tiny new potato to allow for the venting of steam.

TORTILLA PIZZA

- ¼ pound bulk Italian sausage
- 2 tablespoons chopped onion
- 2 tablespoons chopped green pepper
- ⅓ cup pizza sauce
- 1 teaspoon cooking oil
- 1 7-inch flour tortilla
- ⅓ cup shredded provolone cheese
  or mozzarella cheese
- 1 tablespoon sliced pitted ripe olives

In a small nonmetal bowl micro-cook sausage, onion, and green pepper, uncovered, on 100% power for 3 to 4 minutes or till the meat is done, stirring once to break up the meat. Drain off fat. Stir in the pizza sauce.

Preheat a 6½-inch microwave browning dish on 100% power for 2 minutes. Add oil; swirl to coat dish. Place tortilla in browning dish, pressing tortilla to fit the shape of the dish. Spread sausage mixture evenly atop tortilla. Micro-cook, uncovered, on 100% power for 1 to 2 minutes or till heated through. Sprinkle with cheese and olives. Micro-cook, uncovered, on 100% power about 2 minutes more or till cheese is melted. Slide tortilla pizza out onto a plate. Makes 1 serving.

TURKEY REUBEN SANDWICHES

- 2 tablespoons Thousand Island
  salad dressing
- 1 tablespoon dairy sour cream
- 2 teaspoons sliced green onion
- ¼ teaspoon caraway seed
- 2 slices rye bread
- 1 2½-ounce package thinly sliced
  cooked turkey
- 1 2½-ounce package thinly sliced
  corned beef
- ½ of an 8-ounce can sauerkraut, rinsed,
  drained, and patted dry
- 2 slices Swiss cheese (2 ounces)

Stir together Thousand Island salad dressing, sour cream, green onion, and caraway seed. Toast bread slices, if desired. Place bread slices in a shallow baking dish or on a nonmetal platter. In the following order layer the turkey, salad dressing mixture, corned beef, and sauerkraut on the bread slices. Micro-cook, uncovered, on 100% power for 2 to 3 minutes or till heated through. Top each with a slice of cheese. Micro-cook, uncovered, on 100% power about 1 minute more or till cheese is melted. Makes 2 servings.

LAMB CURRY

- ½ pound ground lamb
- ¼ cup chopped onion
- 1 medium tomato, peeled
  and chopped
- 1 small apple, peeled, cored,
  and chopped
- ¼ cup water
- 1 to 1½ teaspoons curry powder
- ½ teaspoon instant beef bouillon granules
- ¼ teaspoon salt
- ¼ teaspoon ground ginger
  Dash garlic powder
- 2 tablespoons water
- 2 teaspoons all-purpose flour
  Hot cooked rice
  Snipped parsley
  Raisins (optional)
  Chopped cucumber (optional)
  Chopped peanuts (optional)

Crumble the ground lamb into a 1-quart casserole. Stir in the chopped onion. Micro-cook, uncovered, on 100% power for 2 to 3 minutes or till the meat is no longer pink, stirring once to break up the meat. Drain off the fat. Stir in the tomato, apple, the ¼ cup water, curry powder, instant bouillon granules, salt, ginger, and garlic powder. Micro-cook, covered, on 50% power for 4 minutes.

Stir together the 2 tablespoons water and the flour. Stir the flour mixture into the meat mixture. Micro-cook, uncovered, on 100% power for 1 to 2 minutes or till the mixture is thickened and bubbly, stirring after every minute. Micro-cook, uncovered, on 100% power for 30 seconds more. Serve mixture over hot cooked rice. Garnish with snipped parsley. Pass raisins, chopped cucumber, and chopped peanuts, if desired. Makes 2 servings.

Lamb Chops: Lamb leg sirloin chops work well in the Lamb and Vegetable Combo. Since they are cut from the sirloin portion of the lamb leg, these chops contain a portion of the hip bone, which varies in shape. This cut differs from lamb leg chops or steaks that are cut from the shank portion of the lamb and contain a round leg bone.

For best results while micro-cooking any type of chop, arrange the meatiest portions of the chop to the outside of the dish and any thinner portions to the inside of the dish. Also, use tongs rather than a fork to turn the chop to prevent the loss of juices.

LAMB AND VEGETABLE COMBO

Pictured on pages 82-83 and the cover—

   2 **4- to 5-ounce lamb chops, cut ½ inch thick**
   1 **tablespoon cooking oil**
   ⅛ **teaspoon dried marjoram, crushed**
      Dash garlic powder
   2 **tablespoons water**
   ½ **teaspoon instant chicken bouillon granules**
   ¼ **teaspoon whole black peppercorns, crushed**
   1 **small zucchini, cut into ½-inch slices**
   1 **small onion, sliced and separated into rings**
   ½ **of a small green pepper, cut into strips**
   1 **medium tomato, cut into wedges**
   1 **tablespoon snipped parsley**

Preheat a 10-inch microwave browning dish on 100% power for 5 minutes. Meanwhile, trim any excess fat from the lamb chops. Add cooking oil to the browning dish; swirl to coat dish. Place the lamb chops in the browning dish. Micro-cook, covered, on 100% power for 1 minute. Turn the chops; micro-cook, covered, on 100% power for 1 minute more. Drain off fat.

Sprinkle the lamb chops with marjoram and garlic powder. Stir together water, bouillon granules, and peppercorns. Pour over the lamb chops in the browning dish. Arrange zucchini, onion, and green pepper around the lamb chops. Micro-cook, covered, on 100% power for 2 to 3 minutes or till the meat is done and the vegetables are crisp-tender. Add tomato wedges. Sprinkle with the parsley. Micro-cook, covered, on 100% power about 30 seconds more or till heated through. Transfer to a serving platter. Spoon juices over meat and vegetables. Makes 2 servings.

STEAK-VEGETABLE POCKETS

   ½ **pound beef top round steak**
   2 **tablespoons cold water**
   1 **tablespoon soy sauce**
   1 **teaspoon cornstarch**
   1 **small carrot, thinly bias sliced**
   1 **tablespoon water**
   ½ **cup broccoli buds**
   6 **fresh mushrooms, sliced**
   2 **tablespoons sliced green onion**
   1 **tablespoon cooking oil**
   1 **small tomato, chopped**
   2 **pita bread rounds**

Partially freeze the beef top round steak. With a sharp knife thinly bias-slice the meat, across the grain, into bite-size strips. In a small bowl or custard cup stir together the 2 tablespoons cold water, soy sauce, and cornstarch; set aside. Place the carrot slices in a shallow baking dish; sprinkle with 1 tablespoon water. Cover with vented clear plastic wrap. Micro-cook, covered, on 100% power for 2 minutes. Stir in broccoli buds, mushrooms, and green onion. Micro-cook, covered, on 100% power for 1 to 2 minutes more or till crisp-tender. Drain; cover and set aside.

Preheat a 10-inch microwave browning dish on 100% power for 3 minutes. Add cooking oil; swirl to coat dish. Add the sliced beef. Micro-cook, uncovered, on 100% power for 2 to 3 minutes or till the meat is done, stirring twice. Stir the soy sauce mixture; stir into the beef. Micro-cook, uncovered, on 100% power for 1 to 2 minutes or till the mixture is thickened and bubbly, stirring every 30 seconds. Gently toss the beef mixture with the broccoli mixture and chopped tomato. Halve the pita bread rounds. Carefully spoon some of the beef-vegetable mixture into each of the 4 pita bread halves. Makes 2 servings.

These bountiful Steak-Vegetable Pockets are quick to prepare when you get home from work.

PORK AND APPLE PIES

2 tablespoons butter *or* margarine
1½ cups corn bread stuffing mix
½ cup water
2 small cooking apples, peeled, cored, and sliced
1 tablespoon water *or* apple juice
½ pound ground pork
2 tablespoons chopped onion
¼ teaspoon dried sage, crushed
¼ cup shredded cheddar cheese (1 ounce)

In a small nonmetal bowl micro-cook butter or margarine, uncovered, on 100% power for 45 seconds to 1 minute or till melted. Toss together corn bread stuffing mix, ½ cup water, and melted butter or margarine. Reserve ½ *cup* of the corn bread stuffing mixture. Firmly press the remaining corn bread stuffing mixture against the bottoms and up the sides of two 15-ounce casseroles; set aside.

In a 1-quart casserole combine sliced apples and the 1 tablespoon water or apple juice. Micro-cook, covered, on 100% power for 3 to 5 minutes or till the fruit is tender, stirring once. *Do not drain.* Stir the apple slices and their liquid into the reserved corn bread stuffing mixture.

In the same 1-quart casserole crumble the ground pork. Stir in the chopped onion. Micro-cook, uncovered, on 100% power for 3 to 4 minutes or till the meat is no longer pink, stirring every minute to break up the meat. Drain off fat. Stir in the apple-stuffing mixture and sage. Spoon the pork-apple mixture into the "crusts" in the individual casseroles. Micro-cook, uncovered, on 100% power for 2 to 3 minutes or till heated through. Sprinkle with the shredded cheddar cheese. Micro-cook, uncovered, on 100% power for 1 to 1½ minutes more or till the cheese is melted. Makes 2 servings.

•
Forming Corn Bread "Crusts": The corn bread stuffing "crusts" for the Pork and Apple Pies are tasty as well as easy to make. Use your fingers to firmly press the corn bread mixture against the bottom and up the sides of each 15-ounce casserole, as shown in the photo. Then, to finish assembling your own individual pies, simply spoon the pork-apple mixture into the "crusts" and top with the shredded cheese.

Meatless One-Dish Meals: Why make a meal meatless? Because meatless foods feature alternate forms of protein that are often quite economical. In addition, main dishes without meat, such as Vegetable Scallop, let you experience different combinations of enticing textures and flavors.

If you occasionally decide to go the meatless route, keep in mind that it is very important to combine vegetable proteins in a way that makes them complete and thus able to fulfill your body's protein requirements. The Vegetable Scallop recipe, for example, blends three different types of cheese, crunchy vegetables, and a nutty topping to give a nutritionally sound and satisfying main dish.

CAULIFLOWER-HAM BAKE

- 1 cup cauliflower flowerets
- 2 tablespoons water
- 2 tablespoons chopped onion
- 1 tablespoon butter *or* margarine
- 1 tablespoon all-purpose flour
- ¼ teaspoon dried basil, crushed
  Dash pepper
- ½ cup milk
- ¼ cup shredded Swiss cheese (1 ounce)
- 1 cup cubed fully cooked ham
- 1 medium tomato, peeled, seeded, and chopped
- 2 tablespoons snipped parsley

Place the cauliflower in a 1-quart casserole. Sprinkle with water. Micro-cook, covered, on 100% power for 3 to 5 minutes or till nearly tender. Drain cauliflower and set aside.

In the same 1-quart casserole micro-cook the onion and butter or margarine, uncovered, on 100% power for 1 to 2 minutes or till the onion is tender. Stir in the flour, basil, and pepper. Stir in the milk. Micro-cook, uncovered, on 100% power for 2 to 3 minutes or till the mixture is thickened and bubbly, stirring every minute. Stir in the shredded Swiss cheese till melted. Gently fold in the cauliflower, ham, tomato, and parsley. Micro-cook, covered, on 100% power for 1 to 2 minutes more or till the mixture is heated through. Makes 2 servings.

VEGETABLE SCALLOP

- 1 cup coarsely shredded cabbage
- 1 cup thinly bias-sliced carrots
- ¼ cup water
- ¼ cup chopped onion
- ¼ cup chopped green pepper
- 1 tablespoon butter *or* margarine
- 2 teaspoons all-purpose flour
- ½ teaspoon instant chicken bouillon granules
- ½ cup shredded mozzarella cheese (2 ounces)
- ¼ cup shredded fontina cheese (1 ounce)
- 2 tablespoons grated Parmesan cheese
- 1 tablespoon toasted wheat germ
- 1 tablespoon sunflower nuts
- 2 teaspoons fine dry bread crumbs

Place the cabbage and carrots in a 1-quart casserole; add water. Micro-cook, covered, on 100% power for 5 to 7 minutes or till the vegetables are tender, stirring once. Drain well, reserving the liquid. Set vegetables aside. Add enough water to the reserved vegetable liquid to measure ⅔ cup total liquid; set aside.

For the sauce, place the onion, green pepper, and the butter or margarine in a 4-cup measure. Micro-cook, uncovered, on 100% power for 2 to 3 minutes or till the vegetables are tender, stirring once. Stir in the flour and bouillon granules; add the reserved ⅔ cup vegetable liquid. Micro-cook, uncovered, on 100% power for 2 to 3 minutes or till the mixture is thickened and bubbly, stirring every 30 seconds.

In the 1-quart casserole stir together the sauce and the shredded mozzarella, the shredded fontina, and the grated Parmesan cheeses till all the cheeses are melted. Stir in the cooked cabbage and carrots. Micro-cook, uncovered, on 100% power for 2 minutes.

In a small bowl or custard cup stir together the wheat germ, sunflower nuts, and bread crumbs. Sprinkle atop the vegetable-cheese mixture. Micro-cook, uncovered, on 100% power for 1 to 2 minutes or till heated through. Makes 2 servings.

INDEX